A note on the paper:
This book is printed on Satimat green 170g/m2 paper, which is made of 60 percent recycled fiber and 40 percent
FSC virgin fiber. Satimat green is a product and registered trademark of Arjowiggins Fine Papers Ltd. Because of
its high recycled-fiber content, this eco-friendly paper reduces consumption of water, energy, and wood.

Front cover photograph: Vegetable cultivation near Timbuktu, Mali

Photography credits

All photographs by Yann Arthus-Bertrand, except:
pages 92–93 © Daniel Schoenen, Freiburg
page 94 © Moore Ruble Yudell, Architects & Planners
page 95 © DR
http://www.vauban.de

All photographs by Yann Arthus-Bertrand are available from the Altitude agency, Paris, France
(www.altitude-photo.com, www.yannarthusbertrand.org).

Library of Congress Cataloging-in-Publication Data:

Delannoy, Isabelle.
Our living Earth : a story of people, ecology, and preservation /
by Isabelle Delannoy ; photographs by Yann Arthus-Bertrand.
p. cm.
ISBN 978-0-8109-7132-5 (Harry N. Abrams)
1. Aerial photography—Juvenile literature. 2. Arthus-Bertrand, Yann. Earth from above—Juvenile literature.
3. Human geography—Juvenile literature. 4. Photographic criticism—Juvenile literature.
I. Arthus-Bertrand, Yann. II. Title.

TR810.D44 2008
779—dc22
2008010324

Originally published in French by Éditions de La Martinière, Paris
English translation copyright © 2008 Harry N. Abrams, Inc.
Translated by Gita Daneshjoo

Photography research: Isabelle Bruneau
Book design: Elisabeth Ferté

Printed and bound in France
10 9 8 7 6 5 4 3 2 1

Abrams Books for Young Readers are available at special discounts when purchased in quantity for premiums
and promotions as well as fundraising or educational use. Special editions can also be created to specification.
For details, contact specialmarkets@hnabooks.com or the address below.

HNA ▇ ▇ ▇

harry n. abrams, inc.

a subsidiary of La Martinière Groupe

115 West 18th Street
New York, NY 10011
www.hnabooks.com

Yann Arthus-Bertrand

Our Living EARTH

A Story of People, Ecology, and Preservation

text by Isabelle Delannoy
illustrations by David Giraudon

Abrams Books for Young Readers
New York

THERE ARE 1.2 BILLION TEENAGERS IN THE WORLD, MORE THAN THE WORLD HAS EVER SEEN!

CHILDREN BORN IN THE POOREST COUNTRIES OF THE WORLD HAVE A 60 PERCENT GREATER CHANCE OF ATTENDING SCHOOL THAN THEY DID 15 YEARS AGO.

THE WORLD IS YOUNG:
1 OUT OF 2 PEOPLE IS LESS THAN 25 YEARS OLD.

90 COUNTRIES IN THE WORLD ARE DEDICATED TO PROVIDING EQUAL ACCESS TO EDUCATION FOR GIRLS.

MORE AND MORE CHILDREN ARE FORMING THEIR OWN ORGANIZATIONS, RADIO PROGRAMS, WORKSHOPS, AND NEWSPAPERS TO HELP OTHER CHILDREN RISE OUT OF POVERTY.

CHILDREN OF THE FUTURE WILL PROBABLY LIVE IN HOUSES THAT PRODUCE ENERGY, RATHER THAN CONSUME IT.

100 MILLION TO 250 MILLION CHILDREN LIVE IN THE STREETS.

THE NEXT GENERATION WILL ALMOST CERTAINLY BE THE ONE TO REAP THE FULL BOUNTY OF SOLAR ENERGY. THE RESERVES ARE VAST: THE EARTH RECEIVES 6,700 TIMES MORE ENERGY FROM THE SUN THAN PEOPLE CONSUME!

THE WORLD

NEVER BEFORE HAVE WE SEEN SUCH HIGH SCHOOL ATTENDANCE RATES. NEVERTHELESS, **MORE THAN 104 MILLION CHILDREN DON'T ATTEND SCHOOL.**

218 MILLION CHILDREN AND TEENS WORK.

MANY LITTLE GIRLS AROUND THE WORLD ARE RESPONSIBLE FOR FETCHING WATER; **THEY WALK AS MANY AS 6 MILES A DAY TO FILL THEIR CONTAINERS.**

A CHILD BORN IN A DEVELOPING COUNTRY IS ON AVERAGE **74 TIMES POORER** THAN A CHILD BORN IN AN INDUSTRIALIZED COUNTRY.

MORE THAN 60 MILLION WOMEN AROUND THE WORLD AGES 20 TO 24 WERE **MARRIED BEFORE THE AGE OF 18.**

NATURAL RESOURCES ARE BEING DEPLETED AND THE CLIMATE IS CHANGING. IF WE DON'T CHANGE OUR LIFESTYLE, THE CHILDREN OF THE FUTURE WILL LIVE ON A VERY DIFFERENT PLANET THAN THE ONE WE LIVE ON TODAY.

90 PERCENT OF THE CHILDREN AND TEENS IN THE WORLD LIVE IN DEVELOPING COUNTRIES.

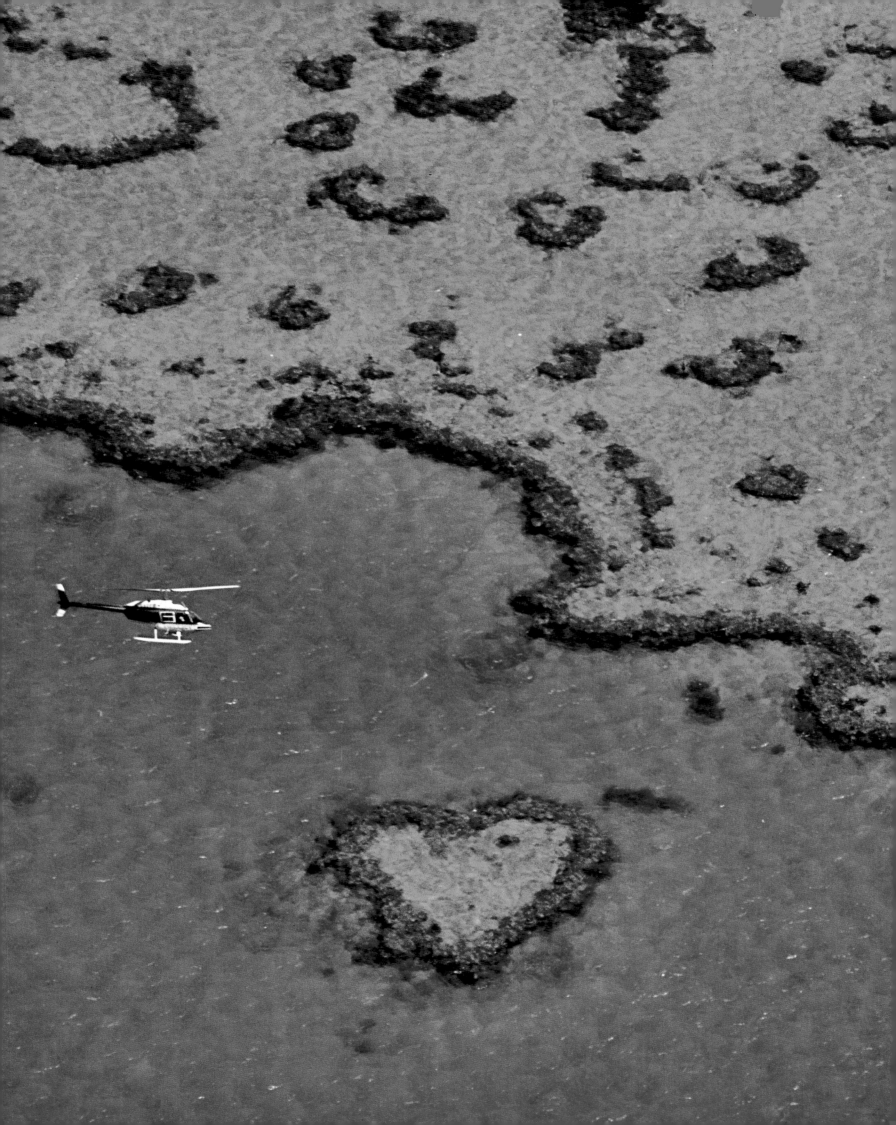

CONTENTS

eat Barrier Reef, Queensland, Australia

OVER THE THIRTY YEARS I SPENT PHOTOGRAPHING THE EARTH FROM ABOVE, I'VE LEARNED THAT OUR LIVES ARE CLOSELY LINKED TO THAT OF THE PLANET.

We depend on water, forests, the land, oceans, and all the living things that surround us. The earth is generous. It offers us immense services. It gives us our food, our water, medicine to heal us, and materials with which we can build, create, trade . . .

Nowadays, we know that we consume more than what the earth can provide. Our lifestyles aren't sustainable; we must find an alternative way to live, ecologically and interdependently. It's possible!

Wondering what to do about our waste? The earth can teach us how to recycle: It's been doing just that for four billion years! Has pollution become a menace? Certain places on earth can filter out pollutants and purify the air and water. Searching for new forms of energy? Just look at plant life! Plants capture energy from the sun and convert it into energy usable by people. Why can't we do the same?

We already know how to build houses in harmony with nature: These houses absorb energy from the sun and soil, and can collect rainwater. This is just one example; you will find many others in this book.

To preserve the earth and our common future, people from all around the world must act together. It's not easy, since for many people in the world, their daily priority is simply to find shelter, a job, or feed themselves and their family. In these pages, you will discover that inequalities, and the gaps in human living conditions, are still immense. I am sure that you will be moved to do something about it, perhaps starting now.

I HOPE THAT IN THE FUTURE, YOUR LIFE ON EARTH WILL RESEMBLE WHAT THE PLANET OFFERS US TODAY: A SUSTAINABLE, ECOLOGICAL, AND LIVING REALITY.

BON VOYAGE !

YANN ARTHUS-BERTRAND
www.goodplanet.org

Schoolchildren in Bobo-Dioulasso, Hauts-Bassins, Burkina Faso

WATER

PART 1

THE **IMPORTANCE** OF WATER IS UNPARALLELED

Two hydrogen atoms, one oxygen atom . . . and life is sustained. Such is the miracle of water. It is a miracle that, up until now, has been observed on only one planet in our universe: Earth. In 4 billion years, ever since the earth was formed, the amount of water on our planet hasn't changed. It's always been the same water that recycles itself, traveling from sea to clouds, clouds to glaciers, and glaciers to rivers. The water that dinosaurs drank millions of years ago is the very water that flows through our faucets today. Since the beginning of time, humankind has been exploiting this precious resource, creating canals to bring it to the fields, digging wells to extract it from the ground, and, in some regions of the world, even succeeding in bringing it directly into homes. Water is indispensable not only to human beings but also to every plant and animal. It's a resource that must be shared. But water is scarce, and our population is rapidly increasing. We are also polluting our waters more and more. Will we ever learn how to conserve water and make it available to every human being—indeed, every living thing?

Camels drinking from a well at Ti-n-Tehoun, Timbuktu, Mali

1.2 BILLION
people do not have access to drinking water

NO LIFE WITHOUT WATER

A well in Fatehpur Sikri, Uttar Pradesh, India

There are millions of species living on the planet, all of which must share this precious resource, water.

These organisms are made mostly of water. An apple, for example, is composed of 93 percent water; a jellyfish, 85 percent; and the human body, 60 percent. A human being can't live for more than 4 days without drinking water. To stay healthy, a person must drink at least 6 cups of water each day. But this resource is scarce. The oceans and seas contain 97.5 percent of the water supply, but because this water is salty, it isn't drinkable. The small percentage of freshwater on Earth is either locked away as ice or confined groundwater. Only 0.01 percent of the water on our planet is available to living things!

VAST INEQUALITIES

• An American consumes an average of 185 gallons each day; a European, 53 gallons; and a Haitian, 5.3 gallons.

• How can a Haitian drink, cook, bathe, clean his home, and wash his clothing with so little water?

• Every person should have access to a minimum of 13 gallons of water per day.

THE HIDDEN WATER WE CONSUME

132 gallons of water to produce 1 pound of wheat

2,642 gallons of water to build a car

5 gallons of water to produce 1 pound of paper

0.66 gallons of water for 0.264 liters of Coca-Cola

Irrigating cornfields near Aigues-Mortes, Gard, France

Every item we produce requires water for washing, rinsing, or freezing. Think before throwing away an item that might still be useful; trade it for something else among your friends, or find a new use for it. Either way, you'll be saving the planet's water!

ttle girls are among the first to be fected by lack of access to water.

A WELL BUILT FOR ATTENDING SCHOOL

Throughout the world, more than 1 out of 6 people walk at least 6 miles a day to fetch water from a well and carry it home. It's often women and young girls who are charged with this task. Their role is vital to their families. But many young girls are so busy fetching water that they don't have the time to attend school. They don't know how to read, write, or count. Imagine how difficult it will be for them to find a job later in life! Some associations have come up with a clever solution: They financed the installation of wells in schools so that these young girls can both bring home water and educate themselves at the same time.

WETLANDS
ARE ENDANGERED

There are many different kinds of habitats. Mountains, deserts, plains, forests, lakes—they all play a role in this great organism that is our earth. As in a human body, when one of the Earth's organs falls ill, the entire body is weakened. The forests and the sea, which lend oxygen to the atmosphere, are the planet's lungs. The lakes, bogs, and swamps are its kidneys. In the body, the kidneys filter out waste products from the blood and eliminate toxins. Similarly, wetlands purify the earth's water and remove toxic elements. They are also a breeding ground for fauna and flora, and the majority of birds in the world depend on them. When these places begin to degrade or disappear, all living things feel the consequences sooner or later. One half of all wetlands have already disappeared. And as for the remaining wetlands, from what diseases do they suffer?

Storks in the Bordj Omar Driss oasis, Algeria

In one century,
HALF OF THE PLANET'S WETLANDS
have disappeared

WHAT ARE WETLANDS?

Elephants in the marshes of the Okavango Delta, Botswana

Abundant plant life, frogs, insects, and birds? This is what we refer to scientifically as "wetlands," where the land and water meet.

They include marshes, swamps, ponds, riverbanks, and bogs. Wetlands are remarkable for their biodiversity, or the diversity of things that live in them. Animals find plenty of food to sustain themselves there, while the dense vegetation provides them with an ideal refuge in which to hide from predators and reproduce. At the end of the day, larger mammals go there to feed. Without wetlands, a number of species would be vulnerable to extinction.

Fish, frogs, insects—like many other birds, the heron finds its sources of food in swamps.

A GARDEN? NO, A PURIFICATION STATION!

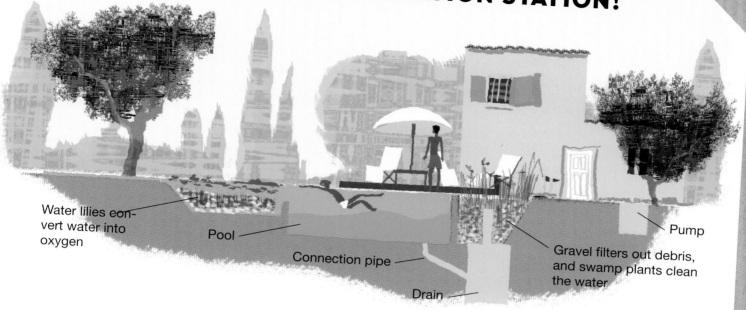

Water lilies convert water into oxygen

Pool

Connection pipe

Drain

Gravel filters out debris, and swamp plants clean the water

Pump

A swimming pool without chlorine? Impossible! Let's re-create the water filtration system in wetlands.

In the world today, an increasing number of communities rely on plants to purify their water, soil, and even the air of their offices and factories. How does it work? Gravel beds filter out debris, while the plants in the swamps ensure the purification of water. For example, the roots of rushes and reeds provide surfaces on which bacteria and mushrooms can filter pollutants. Farther away, other plants, such as irises, enhance purification. Finally, water lilies, which can live in only very clean water, bring much-needed oxygen to the water. Hundreds of different plants can be used in this way! This filtration system can purify the water of a community just as easily as chlorine does a swimming pool.

WHY ARE WETLANDS DISAPPEARING?

Up until a short time ago, humans didn't understand the importance of wetlands. These marshy grounds, swarming with insects, were viewed as harmful, filled with infectious diseases, and therefore essentially useless. This is why humans have slowly destroyed wetlands by draining them to obtain fertile farmland, drying them to enlarge the size of cities, or filling them in to create longer coastlines.

WETLANDS COVER LESS THAN 1 PERCENT OF THE SURFACE OF THE EARTH, YET:

• they provide refuge to more than 100,000 species of animals
• they supply drinking water to 1.5 billion to 3 billion people
• they filter out agricultural and industrial pollutants, such as nitrates, which they can reduce by 80 percent

RIVERS:
FROM THE MOUNTAINS TO THE SEA

In the beginning, rivers start off as springs. They flow for thousands of miles, growing larger as they join with smaller rivers that intersect them, before finally reaching their destination, the sea. En route, they extract minerals from rocks and carry them along to the sea. This is one of the reasons seawater is salty. Rivers and streams are the lifeblood of the majority of freshwater fish, but they are equally indispensable to humans. It is along riverbanks that the world's biggest cities were built. Rivers ensured unfettered access to water for drinking, growing crops, transporting goods, and communicating with other cities. Unfortunately, rivers are livelihoods that humans use and abuse. They divert the course of major rivers and erect gigantic dams. Sometimes, they meddle to such a degree that certain rivers dry up before they reach the sea.

Bends in the Tuul River, south of Lun, Mongolia

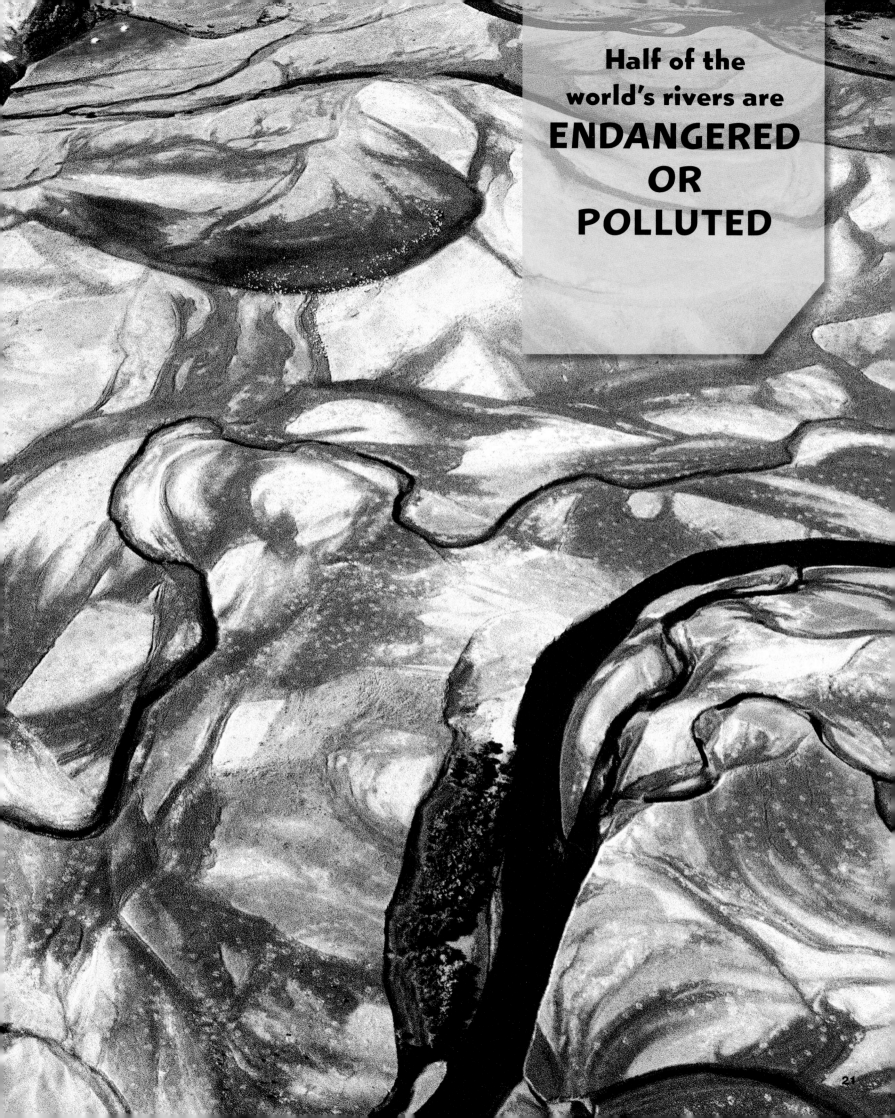

Half of the
world's rivers are
**ENDANGERED
OR
POLLUTED**

21

THE AMAZING FRESHWATER-MAKING MACHINE

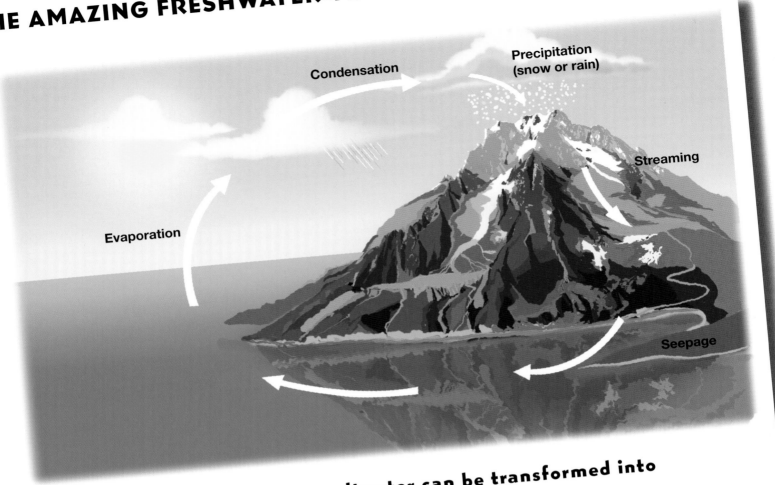

Condensation

Precipitation
(snow or rain)

Streaming

Evaporation

Seepage

With help from solar energy, saltwater can be transformed into freshwater.

When heated by the sun's rays, the saltwater in oceans evaporates, separating from its salt. It becomes invisible freshwater vapor, which rises up toward the sky. Once it reaches the cold layers of the atmosphere, it condenses, appearing before our eyes as clouds. That moisture collects into large drops that eventually fall back to the ground in the form of rain or snow. This precipitation replenishes glaciers and groundwater, which in turn feed springs, streams, and rivers. Over time, their water flows back into the sea and the cycle starts all over again. Thus, the water in the world today is the same recycled water that existed when the earth was formed!

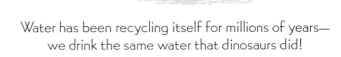

Water has been recycling itself for millions of years—
we drink the same water that dinosaurs did!

RIVERS ARE INDISPENSABLE TO HUMAN ACTIVITY

Dugout canoes in the port of Mopti, on the Niger River, Mali

These pirogues, moored on the Niger riverbank, will soon sail off for a neighboring city, packed with several tons of goods. In Tuareg, the name of the Niger River, *egerou n-igerou*, means "river of rivers."

COMMENDABLE INTERNATIONAL COOPERATION TO SAVE THE NIGER

For the people who make their living from irrigated agriculture, livestock farming, fishing, or river commerce, the Niger is their life. It's also their primary form of transportation. But since 1970, as the climate has been getting warmer, the Niger's flow has slowed. To save this massive river and all the people who depend on it, the governments of 9 riverside countries came together to form the Niger Basin Authority. It's an example that should be followed everywhere to protect the planet's big rivers!

THE NIGER RIVER
MEASURES MORE THAN
2,450 MILES
LONG AND CROSSES 9 DIFFERENT COUNTRIES.

MORE THAN
110 MILLION
PEOPLE LIVE ALONGSIDE THE NIGER.

THE PLANET'S LONGEST RIVERS

• The Nile: 4,132 miles long. Formed by the confluence of the Blue Nile and the White Nile, the Nile River supplies water to all of East Africa, from Lake Victoria to the Mediterranean. It is shared by 9 countries. The Nile was at the source of the great ancient Egyptian civilization, which benefited from many of the river's resources.
• The Amazon: Situated in South America, the Amazon is the second-longest river on the planet. It measures 3,977 miles in length and gave its name to the largest forest in the world, the Amazon rainforest.
• The Yangtze: 3,915 miles long. Emanating from its source in Tibet at an altitude of 21,653 feet, the Yangtze is the third-longest river in the world and supplies China with its water. Today, it is spanned by the immense Three Gorges Dam.
• The Mississippi: 3,710 miles long. This is the longest river in North America and is one of the economic arteries of the United States for industry, agriculture, and transportation.

DAMS: FOR BETTER OR FOR WORSE . . .

The Ohau A hydroelectric plant, South Island, New Zealand

In the twentieth century, people built dams over the majority of the big rivers in the world, as well as a number of smaller ones. Dams block the flow of water and create huge artificial lakes.

These reservoirs are used to supply entire regions and urban centers with water. Dams also generate electricity. Openings built in a dam's walls allow water to break free. As the water falls, it activates turbines that produce electricity, much like a generator on a bike. Dams generate more than 16 percent of the world's electricity!

AT THE BEGINNING OF THE TWENTIETH CENTURY, THERE WERE

600 GREAT DAMS IN THE WORLD. TODAY THERE ARE NEARLY

50,000.

UNEXPECTED ECOLOGICAL AND SOCIAL DAMAGE

A fisherman on Lake Kossou near Bouaflé, Ivory Coast

In the last century, more than

50 MILLION

people were forced to leave their villages due to the construction of dams.

In the artificial lake of the Kossou Dam, dead tree trunks stand as a reminder that this was once a valley with villages and forests. Once, 75,000 people lived there, but they were displaced by the creation of the dam and the irrigation of their valley.

VULNERABLE HUMANS . . .

By making the water more stagnant, dams and irrigation canals foster the growth of populations of mosquitoes, worms, and other creatures that live in only stagnant water. Some of these include dangerous parasites responsible for serious diseases such as malaria; onchocerciasis, an eye affliction that can lead to blindness; and schistosomiasis. In villages bordering the dams, these otherwise rare diseases can develop rapidly, affecting 80 percent of the population.

AND ENDANGERED FISH

These dams also disturb the life cycles of a number species of freshwater fish, which can no longer swim upstream to reproduce. Furthermore, because there is less water, a river's temperature tends to rise, decreasing the amount of available oxygen. Fish often have difficulty adapting.

Of the 10,000 species of freshwater fish studied, 20 percent are endangered or already extinct. In Europe, the rate is closer to 30 percent.

Nowadays, the construction of small local dams is preferred, since they don't disturb the ecosystem as much.

GLACIERS:
GIANTS IN PERIL

So high, so far away . . . and yet so present in the daily life of humanity. Glaciers essentially sustain the lives of half of the world's population, which depends on them for its water supply. Crowning mountaintops, these immense blocks of ice retain water and release it through melting during periods of warmth and dryness. They supply rivers with water during the entire year. The melting of glaciers on a large scale is one of the most visible signs of planetary climate change. The celebrated "eternal snows" of Kilimanjaro will have surely disappeared before 2020. Their surface has already shrunk by 80 percent. Along the mountainsides, streams that only recently were replenished by melting snow are now dry from September to March. River communities no longer have sufficient amounts of water for domestic or agricultural use. In some villages of the region, fighting breaks out over water, pastures, and arable land.

The disappearing snows of Kilimanjaro, Tanzania, in 2006

Inset: Kilimanjaro in 1992

The majority of glaciers in the world could

DISAPPEAR BEFORE THE YEAR 2050

THE EROSION OF GLACIERS IS SPEEDING UP

An eroded iceberg in the Uunartoq Fjord, Greenland

Greenland is a region covered by a layer of ice called an ice cap. This ice cap is extremely thick and heavy and moves slowly from the center of the region toward the sea.

At the coast, it breaks into pieces, creating icebergs. Icebergs are miniscule compared to the ice cap that formed them, but to us, they are immense. Greenland's icebergs are increasing in number. Why? Because today, some of Greenland's largest glaciers are melting 3 times faster than they were 10 years ago. And the melting ice acts like a moving walkway, which destabilizes the ice cap and accelerates its descent toward the sea. This spectacular melting is one of the most obvious signs of present-day climate change.

23 FEET

This number represents the rise in sea level if all of Greenland melted. Low-lying islands, shorelines, and coastal cities would be submerged.

THE HIMALAYAS:
THE SOURCE OF ASIA'S GREAT RIVERS

Mount Everest, Himalayas, Nepal

Glaciers are melting faster than scientists predicted. In Asia, many glaciers in the Himalayas could disappear during the course of this century if climate change isn't stopped. Riverbeds as large as the Ganges, Mekong, and Yangtze could completely dry up during the warm season.

The mesh in gigantic dew nets collects fog water, which accumulates in reservoirs.

FOG-CHASERS

What can a village do when there isn't enough drinking water for all of its inhabitants? It can collect fog. This initiative started in the small village of Chungungo, Chile. Resembling giant spider webs, enormous nets spanning the length of the valley were erected by villagers to catch early-morning dew. The water drips down through the mesh and accumulates in reservoirs for use throughout the village. Nowadays, more than 20 villages harvest "fog water" using this method.

UNPOLLUTED WATER

Throughout the world, nearly 3 children die each minute from diarrhea caused by water pollution. Children from the poorest countries in the world are the most vulnerable, but rich countries are not immune. All over the world, men, women, and children, be they rich or poor, ingest toxic chemicals stemming from agriculture or industry and transported through water. In animals, the consequences of polluted water are already well known. The immune systems of fish, amphibians, and marine mammals become weakened, making them more susceptible to disease. In a number of rivers within industrialized countries, like the Rhône in France, fish are so polluted that it is forbidden to catch and eat them. In other rivers, like the Mississippi in the United States, pollution has reduced the number of fish. Dealing with water pollution is an urgent matter, but how can people help?

Laundry drying on the old bridge of Kayes, Senegal River, Mali

MORE THAN 5 MILLION PEOPLE die each year from illnesses linked to unsafe drinking water or inadequate sanitation

WHEN WATER IS OVERLY POLLUTED, THE SEA DIES

Islet in the Baltic Sea, Porkkala, Finland

THERE ARE MORE THAN 200 "DEAD ZONES" IN THE WORLD

On the water's surface, everything seems normal. But underwater, it's a desert—a "dead zone." These coastal waters are victims of sewage, fertilizers, and other chemical nutrients that stimulate the growth of algae. When algae proliferate extensively, the water becomes deprived of oxygen and can no longer support fish and other marine life. Today, there are more than 200 dead zones worldwide. The largest are in the Baltic Sea, a victim of its landlocked location, and in the Gulf of Mexico, which suffers from extreme pollution in the Mississippi River. In the summer, marine life within several thousand square miles disappears.

75 TO 80 PERCENT OF OCEAN POLLUTION COMES FROM SOURCES ON LAND.

FRESHWATER PLANT AND ANIMAL POPULATIONS ARE HALF THE SIZE THEY WERE 30 YEARS AGO.

ANIMALS ARE THE PRIMARY VICTIMS OF WATER POLLUTION

Seals in the Bay of Somme, France

More than half of all large rivers are extremely polluted.

AT HOME

• Ask your parents to use certified eco-friendly detergents, without surpassing recommended doses.
• Try choosing a vegetable oil–based soap in the shower. It's good for your skin, isn't wrapped in excessive packaging, and is more ecologically friendly than normal shower gels.
• Never pour varnishes, solvents, nonsoluble paint, or used oil in the sink or toilet.

Keep in mind that everything you throw away will one day end up in the sea!

These pollutants originate on land and are transported by rivers. Six million tons of toxic products are dumped into the oceans each year. It's an explosive cocktail filled with many things: pesticides, nitrates from fertilizers, and even phosphates derived from household cleaning products. Some long-banned industrial chemicals, such as PCBs, will not disintegrate. And what about the beauty products that we use on a daily basis and that end up in our sinks, or the pharmaceutical substances in the medicines we take? Daily these create pollution, whose consequences we can't yet fathom.

Oil slicks alone make up 2.5 percent of ocean pollution.

PART 2

FORESTS:
THREATENED PARADISES
OF DIVERSITY

Tropical forests are truly tropical paradises! They contain more than half of the many diverse living things on land. On 2.5 acres alone, one can count 300 species of trees, compared to only several dozen at most in the more temperate forests of Europe, Asia, and North America.

It's hard to guess how many diverse species exist on our planet. Thirteen million? Thirty-five million? One hundred million? Even scientists don't know the answer. At least 2 million have been recorded. Every species is a link in a complex and still not fully understood chain. We human beings are also part of this chain. Like all species, we owe our existence to others: Human beings are part of the biodiversity—the variation—of life-forms on earth. For this reason, we must protect it.

Pink trumpet tree on Kaw Mountain, French Guiana

Tropical forests house at least

HALF OF THE WORLD'S LAND SPECIES

FORESTS: AN INESTIMABLE WEALTH

Village with a small plantation of cacao trees, Man, Ivory Coast

Some local communities in Africa and the Amazon grow cacao, which they sell or trade for other needed goods.

Because cacao trees grow in the shade of larger trees, these people can grow the crop without having to resort to cutting trees. Unfortunately, such methods are falling out of use. Nowadays, many growers resort to clearing the forests of trees to make way for big farms where cacao trees can grow in artificial shade. Some ecological groups, armed with international financial support, hope to reverse this practice and protect the forests where cacao is cultivated.

FOR THREE-QUARTERS OF THE PEOPLE ON THE PLANET, THE FOREST IS THE ONLY PHARMACY.

Forests are an invaluable resource. They provide shelter, firewood, textile fibers, food, and medicine. Three-quarters of people receive medical treatment by way of plants grown in the forest. In pharmacies throughout the industrialized world, the majority of medications are derived from natural sources.

HOW EATING CHIPS CONTRIBUTES TO DEFORESTATION

A new palm oil plantation near Pundu, Borneo, Indonesia

Each year, over
32 MILLION
acres of primary forests are burned or bulldozed.

Forests in Indonesia are victims of the relentless cultivation of palm trees, whose oil is used to produce cookies, chips, and prepared foods, as well as soaps and shampoos.

Soon, this oil could even be used as fuel if we don't do anything to stop it. On the other side of the planet, in South America, the Amazon forest has faced the same fate for the past 40 years. There, deforestation is undertaken primarily to grow soybeans, which are exported to wealthy countries as livestock feed. Protecting the forest means supporting groups who defend it, but also realizing that consuming too much in your own community leads to the destruction of our planet.

PRIMARY FORESTS ARE FORESTS THAT HAVE NEVER BEEN ALTERED BY HUMANS.
THEY CONTAIN EXTRAORDINARILY DIVERSE LIFE-FORMS.

The Tasmanian devil lives in Tasmania: It's an endemic species, meaning it can be found in that region only.

WE ALL DEPEND ON THE FOREST

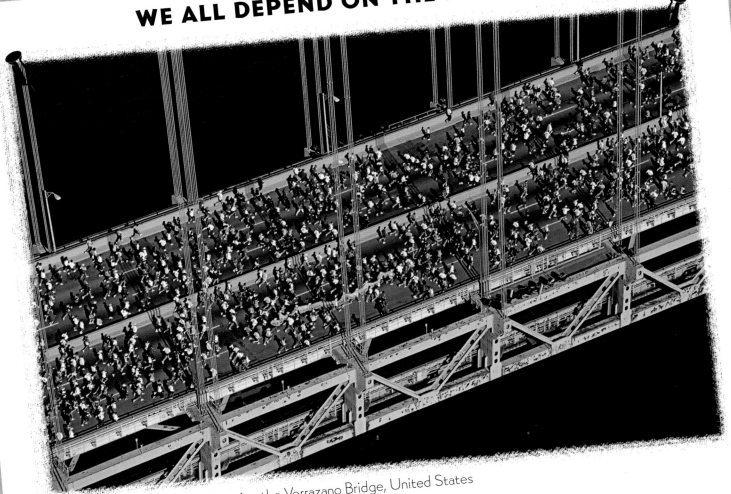

New York Marathon runners crossing the Verrazano Bridge, United States

People, no matter where they live—be it the heart of a big city or the middle of the Amazon—depend on forests. For example, do New Yorkers know that their water is purified in forests located in the northern part of the state?

The mayor's office knows it: In the 1990s, when faced with the delicate question of how to preserve the quality of its tap water, it chose to invest $1.5 billion to protect the state's forests and wetlands (which naturally filter and purify water) rather than build a state-of-the-art purification plant. This plant would have cost the city $5 billion to build and $300 million annually to run and maintain. Thanks to their perceptiveness, New York taxpayers saved themselves $7 billion to $8 billion, and they have quality water!

To study trees, timber rafts are placed along treetops without damaging them.

EVERY FOREST HAS ITS OWN VALUE

Eucalyptus forest near Barberton, Mpumalanga province, South Africa

Whereas a natural forest houses thousands of species, preserves water resources, and mitigates the local climate, eucalyptus plantations are true scourges on the ecosystem.

They soak up so much water and so many nutrients from the ground that their habitat dries up. That's why they're nicknamed "thirsty trees."

One could never hope to replace the incredible diversity contained in a natural forest by building an artificial one. Replanting isn't sufficient and, as we see here, can even be harmful. That's why it's so crucial to protect the remaining primary forests on our planet.

FRANCIS HALLÉ:
ON TOP OF THE FOREST

When he was little, Francis Hallé lived near the French forest of Fontainebleau. Later in life, he had but one dream: to explore the great forests untouched by people—primary forests. But he wanted to study them from above! So how could he climb among the treetops without disturbing the flora and fauna that live there? A plane or helicopter was out of the question. "An architect friend and I came up with the idea of a very light inflatable raft, a 'treetop raft,' that could be placed at the tops of trees without damaging them," he says. The view is spectacular. "Flowers and plants you've never heard of, massive quantities of insects and birds whose cacophony subsides only at nightfall. Yet we might never get to see this incredible sight again. Big industry, helped by the government, is destroying our remaining primary forests. They will have disappeared in 10 to 15 years." Is there still time to save these miracles, which contain so many hidden treasures?

AGRICULTURAL FIELDS

For more than 10,000 years, humans have manipulated their surroundings for the purposes of farming, a practice that has given rise to a great variety of landscapes. Steplike terraces were constructed for farming along mountain slopes; plains are marked by a continuous pattern of hedges and fields; the fringes of the desert resemble a checkerboard with miniscule squares of black, fertile land. By enhancing their environs, farmers have allowed a great number of species to develop and grow. But human creativity didn't stop there. The domestication of several wild species gave rise to hundreds of thousands of animal and plant species adapted to each habitat.

Agriculture has a major role to play in the conservation of biodiversity. Half of the land in Europe, for example, is used for farming. Farmers have tremendous influence on the biodiversity of the continent.

A landscape of brightly colored fields near Sarraud, Vaucluse, France

HALF
THE LAND
IN EUROPE
is controlled
by farmers

HEDGES ARE HAVENS OF BIODIVERSITY

Islands in the Upper Lough Erne, Northern Ireland (Ulster), United Kingdom

In Europe, 3 out of 4 mammals, 1 out of 3 birds, and nearly 1 out of 2 butterflies live among hedges. A one-half-mile hedge is home to an average of 50 birds from 20 to 40 different species. Hedges also serve as shelters for reptiles, frogs and toads, and mammals.

ANIMAL ROUTES

Animals follow the woods and hedges to find their way to plains and hills. For farmers, it can sometimes get expensive to replant and maintain hedges; some communities do their part to chip in and mobilize fellow inhabitants. Farming can only benefit from the maintenance of hedges. Hedges protect crops from wind, and the birds that live in hedges eat many of the insects that would otherwise wreak havoc on crops.

One bird out of three in Europe depends on hedges to survive. Such is the case for the robin.

BEES IN EXILE IN THE CITY

Opéra Garnier in the 9th Arrondissement, Paris, France

Apiarists, those who raise bees for their honey, are sounding a cry of alarm: Bees are dying in droves throughout the world.

They may be victims of pesticides and a growing lack of diversity among flowers, or they may be suffering from a general weakening of their bodies. In California, London, and France, the same conclusion has been reached: Bees are better off in the city than in the countryside! And so today, honey is produced on the rooftop of the Paris Opera, where hives have been installed. Yet in the countryside, farmers have a vital need for bees: 80 percent of crops cannot grow without the help of pollinating bees or similar insects.

FLOWERS AND BEES, 2 LIVES LINKED

For bees and other pollinating insects, flowers are lifeblood: Insects feed on the nectar that flowers secrete from their corolla. When they plunge into the corolla, insects collect pollen, which they carry from flower to flower. Because flowers are immobile, pollination by insects is vital to their reproduction. Pollen is essentially the sperm of the flower, which allows new plants to grow.

"IF THE BEE DISAPPEARED OFF THE FACE OF THE EARTH, MAN WOULD ONLY HAVE 4 YEARS LEFT TO LIVE."
Albert Einstein

THE FATE OF HUMANITY IS LINKED TO THE FATE OF THE OTHER LIVING CREATURES ON THE PLANET.

DESERTS: A FRAGILE LIFE

Desert lands cover one-quarter of the earth's surface. These are dry land areas where freshwater is rare and whose terrain, covered by shriveled vegetation, extends as far as the eye can see. The most arid zones may not receive rain for years on end, and the only water source available to the people who live in them is often nothing more than morning dew. Human beings have succeeded in adapting to the most severe climate conditions by adopting the appropriate lifestyle, crops, and technology. Five hundred million people live in deserts, more than the entire population of the United States. These people—such as Bedouins, Tuaregs, Mongols, and Aboriginals—belong to some of the most ancient human cultures. But in the last century, these lands have become impoverished: People have done more farming, extracted more minerals, and promoted more tourism than these lands could handle. Around 135 million people are at risk of having to leave their desert homes.

Dromedary caravans near Tichit, Mauritania

Deserts cover
25 percent of the
earth's surface, and

**500 MILLION
PEOPLE LIVE
IN THEM**

ANTARCTICA: A DESERT OF WATER

Ice sculpted by the wind at the summit of Mount Discovery, Antarctica

Antarctica, the biggest desert on the planet, contains 70 percent of the world's supply of freshwater!

Antarctica is the most arid desert on the planet. And yet, nowhere else can we find as much freshwater. But the water is frozen, and therefore inaccessible to human beings. The rare species that have acclimated to the area are microscopic. Wind speeds often exceed 180 miles per hour, sculpting the rocks and snow at the summits of the volcanoes, such as on Mount Discovery. A continent of extremes, since 1959 Antarctica has been a world reserve dedicated to peace and science, and so the land doesn't belong to any single country.

THE EMPEROR PENGUIN

Animal species in Antarctica can be found only on the coast of the continent. These include the famous emperor penguins, which settle here by the thousands during the mating season. A male and female penguin produce only one offspring each year. While the offspring is still growing, its mother and father make return trips to the ocean to bring back fish for it to feed on.

The emperor penguin is a species closely associated with Antarctica.

46

ONE-THIRD OF THE EARTH'S SURFACE IS DETERIORATING

Plots of farmland on the outskirts of Tichit, Mauritania

Deserts are expanding all over the planet. In some areas, such as the Sahel and China, desert land is advancing more than several miles per year. Why?

Because when people slash trees, the ground is reduced to dust blown about by the wind. When they extract too much water, fragile ground becomes dry and desolate. When they raise too much livestock on meager supplies of grass, overgrazing weakens the land. There is only one way to stop the advance of deserts: Plant trees, and little by little reclaim the lost ground.

A FRAGILE AND FASCINATING LIFE

To survive in the desert, you have to learn how to save water and shelter yourself from the punishing rays of the sun. Desert plants have adapted by growing very small leaves, such as thorns, or leaves that fold into themselves to prevent being scorched by the sun. Their stems are thick and spongelike, allowing them to store moisture. Camels have light-colored fur so as not to absorb the sun's rays. They stand tall to protect themselves from the heat of the ground. They also store water in their fat. Insects have a thick outer shell and seek out shaded areas in the ground.

PROTECT THE SPECIES!

Four billion years ago, the first forms of life on earth were bacteria. During the course of evolution, they came together to create animals and plants, both of which further evolved. From bacteria to human beings—evolution is an incredible thing. But regardless of whether we're spiders, cacti, whales, or humans, we all share the same genetic code, since we all come from the same bacteria.

Although humans belong to this family, they often destroy other species' habitats and prevent their migration by creating roads, fences, and boundaries. They poach other species, or disturb their natural surroundings by moving them from one part of the world to another. Thus, species die out 1,000 times faster than they would naturally. The earth has already experienced periods of extinction, such as the one in which the dinosaurs disappeared. But for the first time, the cause is linked to a single species: ours. It's up to us to change course.

A whale in Samana Bay,
Dominican Republic

1 out of 4
MAMMALS,
1 out of 3
FISH,
and 1 out of 8
BIRDS
are at risk of
going extinct

LIVING AMONG WILD ANIMALS IS POSSIBLE!

Stag in a park near Copenhagen, Denmark

Deforestation, swamp draining, dam building—human populations are multiplying and claiming more and more of the earth's surface. Within their own environments, wild animals are being deprived of space.

And yet it's possible for us to live in harmony with them. In Denmark, for example, there are a number of wild animals—such as foxes, squirrels, badgers, and stag—that live in parks on the outskirts of the capital, Copenhagen. In Germany, forest preservation has created sanctuaries for the wild fauna of Europe.

WARS KILL ANIMALS TOO

In 2006, hippopotamuses joined the list of endangered species. Their decline is staggering, having occurred over a very short period of time. Hunting is responsible for the decline of 95 percent of hippopotamuses since 1994. But war is also to blame. Poachers, rebels, and militiamen have slaughtered hippopotamuses to eat or sell their meat. When local populations lack the proper resources due to poverty or conflict, they will turn to poaching.

WHEN ONE SPECIES IS THREATENED, OTHERS ARE TOO

Icebergs and Adélie penguins, Terre Adélie, Antarctica

This Adélie penguin in Antarctica seems very much alone on this piece of floating ice! Like one-fourth of the species on earth, it is threatened by climate change.

Rising temperatures imperil its source of food, krill, which is a small shrimplike crustacean that lives in cold water and feeds on algae that forms on ice floes. But because of climate change, ice forms only 2 or 3 times every 5 years. So there is a lot less algae! And therefore, a lot less krill for the penguins to eat. In Terre Adélie, there are half as many penguins as there were 10 years ago.

YOU ARE A PART OF BIODIVERSITY AS WELL!

Human beings are part of the earth's biodiversity. They are mammals: The female, like all female mammals, carries her babies in her womb and breastfeeds them. But humans too often forget that they are living things coexisting with many others. Be it for food, water supply, oxygen, or health, humans are entirely dependent on all the other species on earth. That's why, by not protecting other species, we threaten our own.

CLIMATE CHANGE:
A THREAT TO ONE QUARTER OF ALL SPECIES ON LAND

OCEANS

PART 3

OCEANS ARE INDISPENSABLE TO LIFE

Earth is often called the "blue planet." And not for nothing: 70 percent of the earth is covered by oceans.

Did you know that oxygen, which a great number of species—including our own—depend on, comes in large part from the ocean? Oceans also function as an enormous world thermostat that regulates the climate and enables the planet to be inhabited from the equator to the poles.

The ocean is also an essential source of food for humans. Fishing keeps 1 in 6 people alive. Since 1950, the scales have been thrown off balance: Oceans are being affected by climate change, and the exhaustion of resources is taking a toll. Fish consumption has increased fivefold in the world in only 50 years. That's too much—stocks are being depleted. Where once we thought the ocean was infinite, now we're discovering that it is fragile and sensitive to our actions.

Islet in the Sulu archipelago, Philippines

Oceans cover
70
**percent of
the earth's surface**

THE COASTLINE: AN INVISIBLE OASIS

Nuami Islet, Nokan Hui sand strip, south of the Île des Pins, New Caledonia, France

Two-thirds of the world's coral reefs are in danger of disappearing.

These coral reefs flourish in the shallow, clear waters of tropical coasts. Scientists recently discovered that coral once existed in colder waters as well, along the coastlines of Europe and South America. They lived in deeper water, but their biodiversity was just as rich and varied. Coasts make up only a fraction of marine land, but they boast very rich and varied ecosystems. Plankton, algae, mollusks, fish—coasts house 90 percent of marine life! But two-thirds of the coral on our planet is endangered.

MANGROVES: COASTAL FORESTS

Mangrove forests grow in the water along tropical coastlines. Along with coral, mangroves play a vital role in sustaining ocean life: 90 percent of marine organisms depend on them for shelter in which to reproduce and develop, or because the fish they feed on depend on them. Unfortunately, half of them were razed during the course of the last century.

DID YOU KNOW?
One of the main treatments for AIDS is synthesized from substances produced by a coral sponge of the Caribbean.

MORE THAN HALF OF THE WORLD'S POPULATION LIVES ALONG A COAST

Financial District, Manhattan, New York, United States

The United Nations estimates that in 2025,

75 PERCENT

of human beings will settle along coasts.

However, coastlines represent only

20 PERCENT

of the earth's surface.

People love to settle along coasts. Ports—the doorways to the world—allow for commercial exchange and cultural intermingling.

Coral reefs contain life as rich and varied as that found in tropical forests.

ACTIVE CITIZENS

Each year, the American group Ocean Conservancy organizes an international coastal cleanup day. In 2007, more than 378,000 volunteers from 76 different countries participated in the event. They removed more than 6 million pounds of trash and debris from 33,500 miles of coastline. This work is vital: It has been estimated that 1 million sea birds and 100,000 marine mammals and turtles become entangled in, or are suffocated by, plastic litter each year.

FISHING:
EXCEEDING THE LIMIT

Humans have always depended on oceans for sustenance. They have also always viewed the ocean as an infinite space brimming with unlimited resources. Nowadays, however, we are discovering that the ocean is sensitive to our actions. Fish populations are seriously threatened; species of fish that we only barely knew about have disappeared in the span of several decades. The primary culprit is industrial fishing, whose methods exceed the ocean's limits. Local fishermen around the world are finding it increasingly difficult to do their jobs. A large part of humanity directly depends on oceans for food. The entire marine ecosystem is at risk.

Fishermen returning, Kayar, Senegal

1 OUT OF 6 HUMANS depends on fish for food

90 PERCENT OF FISHERMEN PRACTICE TRADITIONAL AND DURABLE METHODS OF FISHING

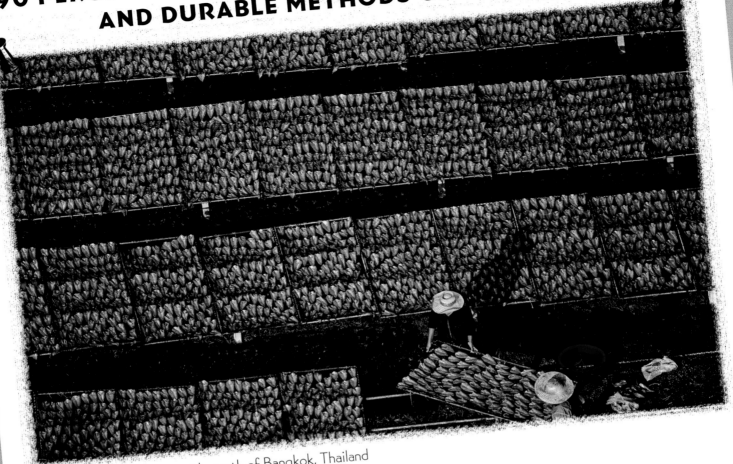

Drying fish in the countryside north of Bangkok, Thailand

Nearly 200 million people, particularly from developing countries, depend on fishing to make a living and as part of their food supply.

Fishing provides these people with a cheap but high-quality source of protein. As seen in this photo, fish are often dried in the sun. Shellfish are gathered during low tide.

WHEN REGULATED, FISHING IS ONE OF THE ONLY SUSTAINABLE INDUSTRIES ON THE PLANET.
BECAUSE FISH STOCKS REPLENISH THEMSELVES.

FISH CAUGHT BY INDUSTRIAL FLEETS ARE OLDER THAN MY GRANDMOTHER!

Emperor fish, grenadiers, and swordfish are examples of fish caught by industrial fleets. They move slowly, and the larger fish are often more than a hundred years old! Over the span of several years, as they arrive on our dinner plates, the populations of some of these species have dropped by more than 90 percent!

TRADITIONAL FISHERMEN ARE THREATENED BY AN UNSUSTAINABLE INDUSTRY

Fisherman, Tunisia

For this traditional fisherman, life is becoming increasingly difficult. Fish populations are being exhausted, and he must travel farther and farther away to find fish.

He is competing against industrial fishing, which is stripping the oceans of marine life. Only 1 out of 10 fishermen is an industrial fisherman, yet they are responsible for half of the world's catch of fish. Their giant boats are equipped with radar and sonar to pinpoint schools of fish. Their enormous nets are dragged down farther and farther to the bottom of the ocean's depths. This kind of fishing isn't sustainable—for marine life, or for fishermen throughout the world.

EMPTYING OUR OCEANS

Industrial fishing poses the biggest threat to our fish supply. Though once thought inconceivable, the tremendous water mass that is the ocean is being depleted of resources.

- **MORE THAN 75 PERCENT** of the fish supply either has been wiped out or is on its way to being so

- **ONE THIRD** of marine fauna is endangered

- **90 PERCENT** of large fish, such as cod, halibut, and tuna, have disappeared

Industrial trawlers come equipped with huge nets that empty the sea of fish.

AQUACULTURE:
CULTIVATING THE SEA

Stemming from the Latin word *ager* (field), "agriculture" means "cultivating the land." But people also know how to cultivate water! This is called "aquaculture." Aquaculture is a flourishing activity: Nowadays, it produces 60 million tons of aquatic organisms, primarily in Asia, up from less than 1 million in 1950. Aquaculture involves the farming of fish, as well as crustaceans, mollusks, and algae. On land, fish are farmed in swamps; in the sea, they are raised in gigantic cages plunged in the water or in tanks along the coast. Mollusks, which feed on marine plankton, are farmed in freshwater regularly cleaned by the tide. Here, bouchot mussels are grown on vertical pilings planted on the coast. And algae offer a number of benefits, both for food and industry.

Mussel farming in Saint-Brieuc Bay,
Côtes-d'Armor, France

MORE THAN
40
PERCENT OF
THE FISH
we consume come
from aquaculture

IS AQUACULTURE A SOLUTION TO OVERFISHING?

Fish farming on Wando Island, Jeollanamdo, South Korea

It takes 7 to 9 pounds of wild fish to produce 2 pounds of farmed salmon.

There are two major types of aquaculture-raised fish in the world. Herbivorous fish, such as carp, feed primarily on algae. Carnivorous fish, such as salmon, sea bass, trout, sea bream, and tuna, feed on other fish. However, farming carnivorous fish won't solve the problem of overfishing in the world. In fact, 7 to 9 pounds of wild fish is required to produce only 2 pounds of carnivorous fish! More sustainable methods of farming are needed to feed fish.

SHRIMP AREN'T ALWAYS ROSY

Shrimp farming is extremely harmful to the environment. The biggest industrial producers of shrimp demolish their natural habitat, mangroves, to build huge concrete tanks in which to raise them. After 10 or 15 years, the water has been pumped so full of antibiotics and pesticides that shrimp farmers have to go elsewhere. As for the mangroves, they are destroyed for good. One way to save mangroves is to avoid eating farmed shrimp!

ALGAE: A PRECIOUS SOURCE OF FOOD

We produce **8 MILLION** tons of algae a year—three-quarters of which are used for food.

Algae harvesting, Bali, Indonesia

Algae are rich in essential minerals, vitamins, and fatty acids. They also produce a gel instrumental to the pharmaceutical and agricultural industries. Consumed in Asian countries since antiquity, algae have many uses that have grown throughout the planet.

Algae can even help counter malnutrition. For example, in Senegal, Guinea, Burkina Faso, and Mali, spirulina, a type of algae grown in small amounts of water, is given to children to alleviate the effects of malnutrition.

In Burkina Faso, spirulina algae is grown in huge vats.

ALGAE IN MY ENGINE?

Will algae refuel the cars of the future? It's quite possible. Much like biofuels derived from palm and rapeseed oils, algae-based fuels are extracted from the oil contained in farmed algae. But algae are even more productive: One acre of algae produces 10 to 30 times more oil than an acre of rapeseed. What's more, because algae are small, they can be grown in suspended tubes, which frees up land for other types of farming.

OCEANS AS CLIMATE REGULATORS

The ocean and atmosphere have had a long history of exchange. Without the ocean, the atmosphere would be deprived of oxygen. Millions of years ago, algae's early ancestors used a process known as photosynthesis to release oxygen into the atmosphere.

Today, microscopic algae, which are part of plankton, still produce 60 to 70 percent of the oxygen in the atmosphere, without which no living thing could survive. By absorbing carbon dioxide (CO_2), oceans mitigate the effects of greenhouse gas emissions produced by humans.

The ocean is like a giant thermostat. It distributes heat throughout the planet and mitigates the temperature fluctuations between winter and summer and between the equator and the poles. But when surface temperatures get too hot, natural disasters such as hurricanes occur, which can destroy nearly everything in their path.

Keys and islands of Exuma Cays, Bahamas

60 TO 70 PERCENT of the oxygen we breathe comes from **OCEAN PLANKTON**

65

THE GULF STREAM: THE OCEAN CURRENT THAT WARMS EUROPE

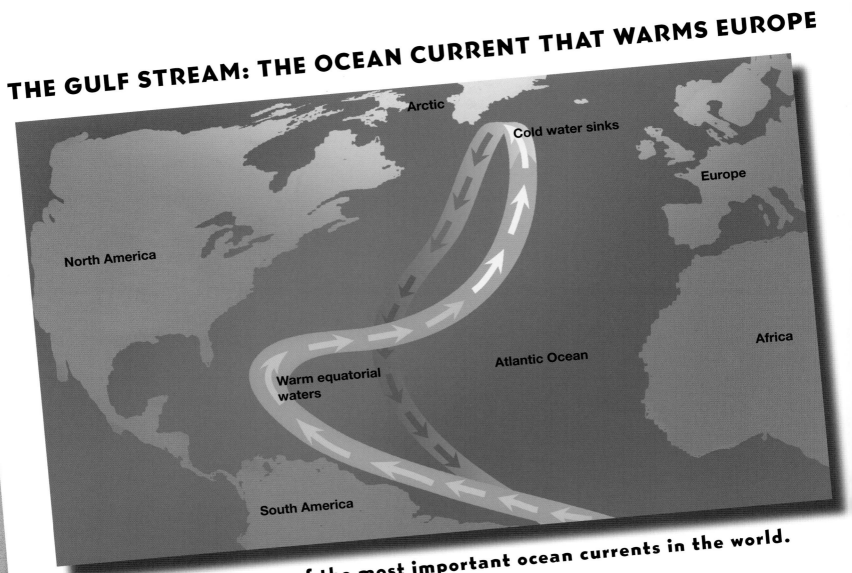

North America

Arctic

Cold water sinks

Europe

Africa

Atlantic Ocean

Warm equatorial waters

South America

The Gulf Stream is one of the most important ocean currents in the world.

It is partly responsible for Europe's temperate climate. Thanks to the Gulf Stream, a city such as Madrid, which is on the same latitude as New York, benefits from a much milder climate.

The Gulf Stream is a warm ocean current that moves warm waters from near the equator to the poles. Think of it like a moving walkway: Gulf Stream waters cool in the icy regions of the poles before being sent back down again toward the equator.

But in the past 50 years, there has been a 30 percent decrease in the quantity of warm water transported by the Gulf Stream. Some scientists believe that this is due to climate change. If the Gulf Stream were to stop flowing, Europe would become bitterly cold.

TROPICS ON THE MOVE

The dotted lines that appear above and below the equator on a world map indicate the Tropic of Cancer to the north and the Tropic of Capricorn to the south.
Scientists at NASA have observed that these tropic "lines" have moved nearly 70 miles toward the poles! Locally, this disrupts the rhythm of rainfall and expands dry regions in Australia, the American West, and the Mediterranean. Here, too, climate change is thought to be the culprit.

WHEN THE OCEAN WARMS UP, HURRICANES ARE MORE LIKELY TO FORM

The northwest quarter of New Orleans, near Lake Pontchartrain, after Hurricane Katrina swept through in September 2005, Louisiana, United States

The force that devastated these homes and thousands around them came from the ocean. When the water's surface temperature is too high, energy is released into the atmosphere, forming powerful whirlwinds that rise up toward the sky: These are hurricanes.

Cyclones have become more intense and more frequent over time due to climate change.

THE OCEAN ABSORBS CO₂

Water has a natural ability to absorb carbon dioxide. The colder the water, the better it is at dissolving significant quantities of CO_2. This is how oceans mitigate the effects of greenhouse gases and rising temperatures. But if the ocean keeps getting warmer, it can no longer perform this essential role. Yet another problem is that CO_2 acidifies the ocean and endangers certain species of plankton, whose shells are sensitive to the acidity.

PART 4

LAND

DON'T THROW AWAY GARBAGE!

The mountains of waste stemming from production and consumption encumber our societies a bit more each day. Not only is our population rapidly increasing and consuming more and more, but we manufacture industrial products that aren't made to last, so we discard, buy again, and discard once more—a lot faster than the planet can handle. The result? Our waste is accumulating. Rich countries, not knowing what to do with it all, send it by the boatload to developing countries. Used paper, computers, game consoles, and other kinds of electronics are shipped away. In poorer countries, waste is recycled, but often under bad conditions that can endanger workers' health, as some products contain a number of toxic substances. They can also contaminate the air, soil, and sources of drinking water. Today, we must rethink our patterns of consumption and production with a view to making them more sustainable. Our unwanted items should be treated as materials to recycle, not as waste that must be immediately disposed of.

Open-air waste dump, Santo Domingo, Dominican Republic

In industrialized countries, the volume of trash per inhabitant **TRIPLED** in the last 20 years

EACH PERSON IN A DEVELOPED NATION GENERATES HUNDREDS OF POUNDS OF WASTE A YEAR

Automobile scrap yard, Saint-Brieuc, Côtes-d'Armor, France

A COMPUTER
generates a total of 3,307 pounds of waste

A GOLD RING:
440 pounds of waste

A CELL PHONE:
165 pounds of waste

To improve your consumption patterns, it's best to buy only those objects you need most and rent those you don't use as often (a drill, wallpaper stripper, DVD player, car . . .). Splurge on high-quality products that last longer and repair them instead of throwing them away.

When thrown in the proper bin, aluminum can be recycled.

AN ACCUMULATION OF PLASTIC DEBRIS IN THE HEART OF THE PACIFIC

In the Pacific Ocean between California and Hawaii, in an area where a number of ocean currents converge, a heap of discarded plastic objects was found: Plastic bags, toothbrushes, toys, and cups had accumulated on a surface area larger than the state of Texas! If nothing is done about it, it will remain there for a long time: Plastic takes several hundred years to decompose.

NATURE HAS BEEN RECYCLING FOR 4 BILLION YEARS

Autumn forest, Charlevoix region, Quebec province, Canada

When the leaves of these trees fall to the ground, they will decompose, much to the delight of the bacteria, mushrooms, and small insects that will make them their primary source of food.

These, in turn, produce minerals, which become the primary nutrients for plants and trees. Everything is recycled. Nothing is lost. We should all be inspired by this natural cycle, in which every bit of waste is a resource for something else.

GOLDEN RULES TO FOLLOW EVERY DAY:

- Choose recyclable products over wasteful ones: Use cotton napkins and ceramic plates instead of paper ones, avoid using disposable towelettes, and opt for reusable drinking containers instead of plastic bottles.
- Steer clear of overpackaged products, meaning those with several layers of packaging.
- Avoid buying individually wrapped products; shop for bulk items instead.

ONE-FOURTH OF THE WEIGHT OF TRASH,
AND, FOR EVERYDAY PRODUCTS,
20 TO 60 PERCENT OF THEIR PRICE!

LIMITED MINING RESOURCES

Unlike energy sources, the supply of primary metals such as copper, aluminum, and nickel hardly ever gets any attention. However, reserves of these metals will likely be used up by the end of the twenty-first century.

During the course of the twentieth century, thanks to powerful techniques, we extracted large quantities of metals. Extracted metals enjoyed a surplus, so their prices dropped considerably. But newly industrializing countries, such as China and India, could cause metal consumption and prices to rise. After all, the earth's resources are not inexhaustible.

In addition, our needs are changing. We are using more and more high-tech items such as computers, telephones, and high-definition screens. The construction of these items requires a number of metals whose reserves are already being depleted.

So let's try to change our habits: We must make an effort to recycle and reuse, rather than continually extract and discard.

Open-air coal mine near Delmas, South Africa

If they're not recycled,
THE WORLD'S METAL RESOURCES could run out within the next century

MINING POLLUTES THE ENVIRONMENT: THE EXAMPLE OF URANIUM

Uranium mine in Kakadu National Park, Northern Territory, Australia

Uranium mining entails the hauling away of enormous quantities of rocks: Nearly 1.4 tons of ore are needed to obtain 1 pound of pure uranium. Uranium serves as fuel for the production of electricity in nuclear power plants.

The dust and debris that ensues from mining can pollute the environment. In this Australian mine, huge sprinklers spray water in the immediate area around the mine to suppress airborne dust, forming strange rings on the edge of the Kakadu marshes.

This energy source is heavily disputed, because it produces radioactive waste that remains dangerous for thousands, even millions, of years.

There are only 60 years of uranium reserves left on the planet for nuclear power plants to use.

ALUMINUM: AN EXAMPLE OF RECYCLING

It takes 20 times less energy to recycle aluminum cans than it takes to produce them. What's more, because aluminum doesn't lose its original quality, it can be recycled over and over again. Due to sorting errors, only half of the aluminum cans in Europe are recycled—a pity, given that a nonrecycled can takes 10,000 years to decompose in nature!

ELECTRICAL APPLIANCES: A MINE OF METAL TO RECYCLE

Scrap metal yard, Aspropyrgos, Attica, Greece

Metals are used in the production of household appliances as well as in high-tech items. A computer or cell phone contains around 30 different metals. For the most part, these are rare and precious metals such as gold, tantalum, germanium, indium, and platinum, which we don't know much about but use every day.

Recycling is crucial to avoid a shortage of these metals. Avoid throwing high-tech appliances in the garbage, because the metals they contain are toxic waste. Once these appliances have stopped working, they must be taken back to the store or to a special waste reception center.

IN THE DEMOCRATIC REPUBLIC OF CONGO, COLTAN MINING IS DETRIMENTAL TO HUMANS AND GORILLAS

Columbite-tantalite, or coltan, contains tantalum, a rare and precious metal used in the production of computers, cell phones, portable music players, and video game consoles. One of the countries where coltan is most plentiful is Congo. Located in the tropical forests, coltan deposits are at the center of a veritable war between government forces and rebels. Humans aren't its only victims. Gorillas are hunted down to feed coltan miners, and half of their population has already disappeared from the region.

OIL:
A RARE RESOURCE

In the span of 50 years, oil has taken control over every aspect of daily life in industrialized countries: We depend on our cars to get around; our goods—now manufactured on the other side of the planet—are sent to us by truck, airplane, and cargo ship; our food is grown thanks to tractors; our homes are built with cranes; our resources are extracted by bulldozer; and so on. And plastic objects, which are directly derived from oil, are everywhere in our houses, offices, and factories.

Because our lifestyle centers around oil, we have no option but to constantly seek out more oil reserves. But today, we consume more oil than we find. This resource is becoming rarer, and therefore more expensive. Finding ways to consume less oil, or finding alternatives to it, is crucial to the health of our planet.

Al Shaheen oil platform, Qatar

We consume 2 TO 3 TIMES MORE OIL than we discover

WHAT WILL WE BE DRIVING IN THE FUTURE?

Mopeds near Bangkok, Thailand

Who needs a big car to get around?

For some trips, such as from home to work, shared transportation or two-wheelers, like these mopeds, are certainly more economical than driving a car. Because of gas shortages, cars are becoming smaller and smaller, and some hybrid vehicles operate using 2 power sources: fuel and electricity.

MORE SHARED TRANSPORTATION

In the future, shared transportation will be more widespread thanks to city trams and commuter trains. We'll also be able to share bikes, and even cars, from designated stations throughout the city. These schemes already exist in Europe. In Geneva, for example, more than 60,000 people no longer own their own car; they have access to publicly available cars that they drive according to need. Because not everybody needs a car at the same time, this scheme is very economical.

Over short distances, goods will increasingly be transported by train or boat.

BIOFUELS: AN ECOLOGICAL ALTERNATIVE TO OIL?

Deer in the Chevreuse Valley, Yvelines, France

A car emits 50 percent MORE POLLUTANTS over short distances.

For short trips, it's better to travel by foot or bike than by car. Each year, a car emits on average 3 times its weight in pollutants.

Alcohol (from sugarcane, corn, or beets) and oils (from palm or rapeseed) are powerful enough to serve as fuel. We call them "biofuels."

But are these alternatives ecological? The majority of them still aren't, because growing the plants they are derived from requires plenty of land. Finding this land means clearing forests in Indonesia for the production of palm oil, or in the Amazon to grow sugarcane. Moreover, with 850 million hungry people in the world, why use farms to produce fuel instead of growing food?

Forests, such as this one in the Amazon, are razed in order to produce more biofuel.

RENEWABLE
ENERGY SOURCES

Swimmers in Grindavik, Iceland, enjoy water heated directly by the planet. In fact, this country sits astride the Atlantic rift, where the earth's crust is very hot. This heat is called geothermal energy (from *geo*, meaning "earth," and *thermos*, "heat"). Geothermal energy varies around the world, but it is always usable, most notably for warmth. It is but one of the many clean energy sources that we don't use enough. Solar energy, for example, can be collected by panels and converted into heat or electricity. Wind energy is harnessed by windmills. The power of tides can even produce electricity. These forms of energy are inexhaustible and don't emit greenhouse gases. They are being developed all over the planet and will surely be among the energy sources of the future.

Blue Lagoon, near Grindavik, Reykjanes, Iceland

Nowadays,
RENEWABLE ENERGY SOURCES are the fastest-developing energy sources in the world

THE NEW MILLS: WIND TURBINES

The central windmill of Avignonet Lauragais, Haute-Garonne, France

This village makes good use of its windy plains to produce electricity generated by wind turbines.

In France, their installation has been slow, but in a number of other regions in the world, wind turbines are being developed rather quickly. In the United States, the number of wind turbines increased by half in the year 2007 alone.

Wind turbine blades capture wind and drive it through the rotor. As with a bicycle generator, this rotating movement produces electricity. The larger the blades, the more powerful and quiet they are.

PRODUCING ENERGY THROUGH WASTE: BIOGAS

The food thrown away in our trash cans, as well as industrial and agricultural food matter, can be broken down by bacteria and transformed into a gas we call "biogas." Biogas can be used to heat homes, produce electricity, and even run buses.

TURNING THE SUN'S ENERGY INTO ELECTRICITY

Thermoelectric solar panels in Sanlúcar la Mayor, near Seville, Andalusia, Spain

Like a sunflower, this solar energy plant orients its photovoltaic panels toward the sun in order to harness the maximum amount of its energy. Sensors in the panels generate a high level of energy from sunlight, which produces electricity.

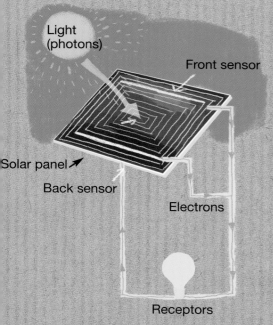

Light (photons)

Front sensor

Solar panel

Back sensor

Electrons

Receptors

Sensors placed in panels convert energy from the sun's rays into electricity.

WHY DOESN'T WOOD-BURNING HEAT CONTRIBUTE TO THE GREENHOUSE EFFECT?

Wood is used quite often for heating. This energy source is technically called "biomass wood." When it originally comes from forests that have been planted and maintained using sustainable methods, biomass wood is a renewable energy source that is a "carbon neutral" fuel. Why? To produce its wood, a tree must absorb carbon dioxide from the atmosphere. Thanks to the solar energy harnessed by its leaves, the tree separates the carbon and oxygen and stores the resulting organic carbon in its trunk, leaves, and branches. So when we burn wood, we're merely releasing the carbon that the tree absorbed several years earlier, which is neutral for the atmosphere.

PART 5

CITIES

AN URBAN
MILLENNIUM

Humanity is undergoing a revolution: Since the beginning of history, humans have made their homes in the rural areas and countryside where they grew their food; today, however, the majority of people live in urban areas. And that changes a lot. In the city, food isn't grown next door; it must be brought in. The same goes for drinking water. But trash must be taken out. Industrialized countries, such as those in Europe, or the United States, have already experienced this urban revolution, but it occurred at a slow pace. Nowadays, the urbanization of developing countries is occurring very rapidly. And it's not without its consequences: poverty, unemployment, increasing crime, and drug use—the problems are numerous. Environmentally speaking, water quality has worsened, groundwater sources have become impoverished, and the air has become more polluted. But cities are also places of great excitement and dynamism. They generate more than half of the economic wealth of poor countries and up to 85 percent in richer ones. The challenges introduced by galloping urbanization are considerable, but they're far from insurmountable.

City of Lignon, Geneva, Switzerland

Since 2007,
MORE THAN
1 OUT OF 2
HUMANS
LIVE IN CITIES

THE WORLD'S GREATEST MEGALOPOLISES

Shinjuku district, Tokyo, Japan

In 1950, only the population of New York City exceeded 10 million, earning it the title of "megalopolis." In 2000, there were 19 megalopolises in the world, primarily located on the continent of Asia. Tokyo, the capital of Japan, is the biggest: It is home to nearly 30 million people.

IF EVERYONE ON EARTH LIVED LIKE AN AMERICAN, WE'D NEED 6 PLANETS TO SUPPORT THEM ALL. IT'S IMPOSSIBLE!

DO YOU KNOW YOUR ECOLOGICAL IMPACT?

The measurement of your home or apartment is not the actual amount of space that you occupy on earth. You must also factor in the space required to produce your food, manufacture your belongings, and eliminate your trash.

Each human being requires slightly less than 5 acres of land to meet his or her needs.

HOW CAN WE FEED OUR CITIES?

Greenhouses in San Augustin, near Almeria, Spain

How do we feed the hundreds of thousands of people who live in cities? By moving agriculture elsewhere. In Spain, greenhouses extend as far as the eye can see.

Housed under plastic roofs, fruits and vegetables grow very quickly, without even needing to be rooted to the ground. The roots of these plants are bathed in trays filled with a nutritional solution combining water and mineral salts. The tomatoes, cucumbers, peppers, and more that are grown there end up in the supermarkets of cities throughout Europe. However, this kind of separation between highly productive agriculture and heavily consuming cities isn't sustainable. We must reinvent intermediaries that can once again link cities with the land.

In the winter, tomatoes are often grown industrially in enormous greenhouses.

THE PERCENTAGE OF THE POPULATION LIVING IN CITIES AROUND THE WORLD WAS:

2 PERCENT IN 1800

30 PERCENT IN 1950

MORE THAN 50 PERCENT SINCE 2007

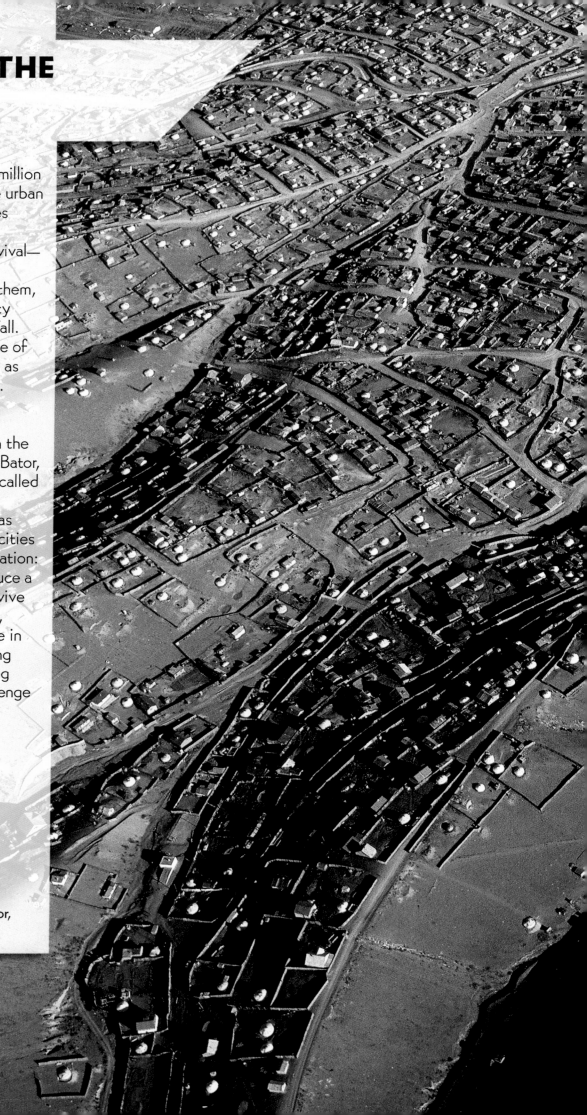

MOVING TO THE CITY

Each week, more than 1 million people are added to the urban population. Poor, rural families migrate to cities in order to increase their chances of survival—either their patch of land has become too small to sustain them, or they are driven into poverty when the prices of produce fall. Sometimes, they flee because of environmental problems, such as soil erosion or desertification. Thus, in Mongolia, nomads confronted with steppe desertification seek refuge in the outskirts of the capital, Ulan Bator, where they plant their tents, called yurts. They form incredible shantytowns that are known as yurt districts. The growth of cities also occurs through overpopulation: In poorer cities, families produce a lot of offspring. Trying to survive in a climate prone to violence, avoiding the spread of disease in areas without drains or drinking water, finding a school, gaining employment—it's a daily challenge for the billion people living in shantytowns.

Yurts on the outskirts of Ulan Bator, Mongolia

More than
**1 MILLION
PEOPLE**
leave the
countryside
each week

MORE THAN 1 OUT OF 7 PEOPLE LIVE IN A SHANTYTOWN

Favelas in Rio de Janeiro, Brazil

The houses are made of sheet metal or pasteboard, there's no plumbing, trash isn't removed, and there are few schools—such is life in shantytowns, where, globally, a billion people live. Their inhabitants are more susceptible to hunger, get sick more often, and have less chance of finding work than people living in more favorable areas. In these conditions, violence occurs more often. Women are the primary victims: They are subjected to violent aggression 2 times more often than men.

GEETA, A STREET CHILD IN MUMBAI (BOMBAY), INDIA

In Mumbai, India, 100,000 people live in the streets in makeshift houses of cardboard, wood, or sheet metal. Geeta is one of them; she shares the family hut with her parents, two younger sisters, and brother. "But don't go thinking that my parents don't work," Geeta says. "My mother does the housework, and my father takes the children to school." But the public school didn't accept her because she doesn't have a home.

One day her mother joined Mahila Milan ("women together" in Hindi), which encourages women to come together and save their money to purchase a home and exercise their rights. Today, Geeta works for the association. She helps women living in the street to find a real apartment, with running water and plumbing.

HARD WORK FOR YOUNG PEOPLE

Las Purgas Market, Santo Domingo, Dominican Republic

Life is difficult for the youth of the world. They are 3 times more likely to be unemployed than adults. The lack of opportunity and underemployment pushes millions of young people from rural areas to cities in search of a better life.

Many of these young people work outside of any legal jurisdiction. This is called the "informal sector." It includes 75 percent of the Dominican Republic's workforce.

YOUNG PEOPLE CONSTITUTE NEARLY HALF OF THE WORLD'S UNEMPLOYED WORKERS.

Low-paying, menial jobs are the only work available to many young people around the world.

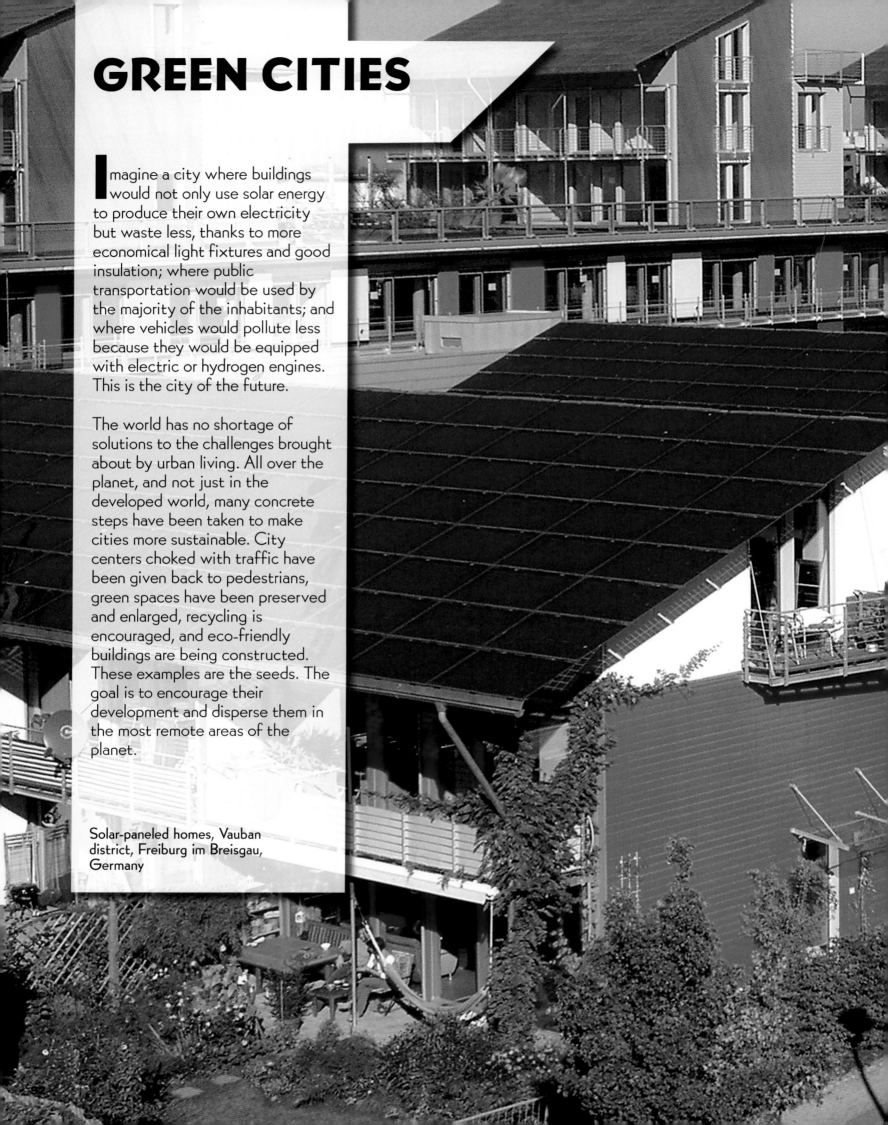

GREEN CITIES

Imagine a city where buildings would not only use solar energy to produce their own electricity but waste less, thanks to more economical light fixtures and good insulation; where public transportation would be used by the majority of the inhabitants; and where vehicles would pollute less because they would be equipped with electric or hydrogen engines. This is the city of the future.

The world has no shortage of solutions to the challenges brought about by urban living. All over the planet, and not just in the developed world, many concrete steps have been taken to make cities more sustainable. City centers choked with traffic have been given back to pedestrians, green spaces have been preserved and enlarged, recycling is encouraged, and eco-friendly buildings are being constructed. These examples are the seeds. The goal is to encourage their development and disperse them in the most remote areas of the planet.

Solar-paneled homes, Vauban district, Freiburg im Breisgau, Germany

Since **2000,** **ECO-COMMUNITIES** **have been** **flourishing** **around the world**

100 PERCENT OF THE ENERGY SOURCES ARE RENEWABLE

Bo01 Tango Housing, Malmö, Sweden

This eco-community was once an old industrial area that had been particularly affected by factory closings. In 1990, Malmö decided to come out of its economic crisis by betting on ecology.

This eco-community is made up of individual homes and office buildings, apartment buildings, businesses, and residences reserved for people under 25 and over 55. Each building must follow one common rule: It must be in direct contact with water and nature.

The community's energy sources are 100 percent renewable thanks to a system combining solar, wind, and geothermal energy, as well as energy stemming from the fermentation of waste products. And when it generates too much electricity, neighboring areas reap the benefits!

IN BEDZED, LONDON'S FIRST ECO-COMMUNITY, HEATING HAS BEEN REDUCED BY 90 PERCENT, TOTAL ENERGY CONSUMPTION BY 70 PERCENT, AND THE VOLUME OF WASTE BY 75 PERCENT!

THE ECO-COMMUNITY OF VAUBAN IN FREIBURG, GERMANY

Vauban district in Freiburg im Breisgau, Germany

Each year,
8,000 TO 10,000 VISITORS
from around the world come to Vauban to learn about its energy-saving methods, eco-urbanism, and renewable energy sources.

With its plant-based roofing, solar panels, and pedestrian-dominated streets, the eco-community of Vauban in Freiburg is a pioneer in eco-construction.

There, homes are "passive," meaning that they heat themselves entirely by the sun's rays, ground heat, and especially by not losing their interior heat. The rehabilitation of the community is primarily due to the sheer will of its inhabitants, who put all their weight behind certain key decisions: to respect existing trees, limit energy consumption, create more green spaces, and even construct a collective bread oven!

A GREEN CITY IN THE MIDDLE OF THE DESERT?

The emirate of Abu Dhabi, one of the world's principal exporters of oil, joined forces with the World Wildlife Fund to construct a model green city called Masdar ("the Source").

The city, which will be built according to local architectural traditions, will protect the area's flora and fauna and will live on local sources of food. Masdar will be the world's first zero-carbon, zero-waste, car-free city!

PART 6

PEOPLE

HOW MANY ARE WE? HOW MANY WILL WE BECOME?

Two thousand years ago, there were about 250 million individuals on the planet. Today, that's only slightly more than the number of people who live in Indonesia (230 million inhabitants). The human species is living through a time of demographic explosion: Today our population is 6 billion, and it will grow another 3 billion before the year 2050. Yet the divisions between rich and poor among the earth's inhabitants are substantial. On the one hand, a significant portion of the world's young and poor live in developing countries; on the other, a rich and aging minority lives in industrialized countries. In order to live together on this limited planet, not only must we rethink our patterns of production and consumption, but we must also combat inequality, share access to resources, and offer young people—the world of tomorrow—better hopes for the future. Peace will come at this price, and sustainable development isn't possible without it.

Love Parade, Tiergarten Park, Berlin

6.6 BILLION people in 2007, **9 BILLION** in 2050

THE WORLD IS YOUNG

Rubber tracks on a playground, near Doha, Qatar

One out of two human beings is less than 25 years old. But childhood and adolescence aren't experienced the same way throughout the world.

The differences between young people living in rich countries and those in poor countries are considerable. In poorer countries, inhabitants have less access to food, water, medical treatment, electricity, transportation, information, and culture. Youth are the most deprived. Many have left the countryside for the cities. Making ends meet is the name of the game, with young people looking for odd jobs as opportunities arise. Lured by the wealth of industrialized countries, some of them choose to emigrate.

IF THE WORLD WERE A VILLAGE OF 100 INHABITANTS . . .

- 60 would live in Asia
- 14 in Africa
- 11 in Europe
- 9 in Latin America
- 5 in North America
- and fewer than 1 in Oceania

A FULL 90 PERCENT OF CHILDREN AND ADOLESCENTS IN THE WORLD LIVE IN DEVELOPING COUNTRIES.

CHILDREN AREN'T BORN EQUAL

School in Clichy-sous-Bois, Seine-Saint-Denis, France

Born in Europe, these children can expect to live, on average, until the age of 75, even 80. They will benefit from free schooling, medical treatment, and cultural services such as libraries and exhibitions, even if their families live on modest means.

The same goes for many developed countries. But it's very different for children born, for example, in Swaziland, in southern Africa: Their life expectancy is only 30 years. The children in this country most likely work for a living, rather than play in school courtyards. Swaziland has the lowest life expectancy in the world. At an age when some people in developed countries have their first child, those in less developed countries face death.

UNACCEPTABLE GAPS IN WEALTH

Eighty percent of the wealth in the world is held by 15 percent of the planet's inhabitants. The world is becoming richer, but inequality is growing. The wealth gap and unequal access to resources are at the source of tensions and conflicts.

PLANET-WIDE INEQUALITY
FOR WOMEN

Sustainable development cannot be achieved without equality among all human beings. Today, persistent inequality between men and women is one of the most glaring forms of injustice in the world. Many women are still illiterate, and too many young girls are not educated. Even in countries where equality between men and women is guaranteed by law, discrimination persists. Women are often paid less than men and struggle to get promoted. Yet women play a critical role in achieving sustainable development. It's the women of the family who provide children with food, water, healthcare, and education: They are at the heart of the connection between resources and the needs of us all. Today, we know that the countries that overcome poverty and succeed in stabilizing their populations are those that make women's education and their rights a priority.

Cotton sheets drying in the sun in Jaipur, Rajasthan, India

Women perform two-thirds of the work in the world, **BUT THEY ONLY EARN A TENTH OF THE REVENUE**

IN MANY CULTURES, GIRLS GET MARRIED BEFORE THE AGE OF 18

Cotton harvest on the outskirts of Banfora, Burkina Faso

Local traditions can prompt families to marry off their daughters at a young age—sometimes even before they turn 10 years old.

At that age, it's difficult for a young girl to express her opinion and rebel against her parents' wishes. Her entire life changes overnight. When she marries too young, a girl risks having a dangerous pregnancy or dying during delivery. Fortunately, education for girls is progressing worldwide. And the more a girl is educated, the more options she will have.

WOMEN DEPRIVED OF THEIR ASSETS

In a number of regions throughout the world, particularly in sub-Saharan Africa, women are denied property rights. Thus, if a woman is widowed or divorces, she risks losing her home, land, livestock, and possessions. This form of discrimination is the result of a tradition that favors men in terms of inheritance and property. But this tradition is also supported by laws that, in certain countries, don't treat men and women as equals when it comes to divorce and inheritance.

IT IS MOSTLY EDUCATED WOMEN WHO PULL THEIR FAMILIES OUT OF POVERTY.

IN RICH COUNTRIES, WOMEN'S SALARIES ARE, ON AVERAGE, 15 TO 20 PERCENT LOWER THAN THOSE OF MEN

Roof terrace, Congress Center Auditorium, Monte Carlo, Monaco

Born in the same European country and belonging to the same generation, this man and woman benefit from the same educational opportunities and enjoy the same rights. However, he probably holds a higher position in his firm than she does in hers. Even if they perform the same functions, he probably has a higher salary than she does. What's more, women are more often victims of poverty, especially when they are single mothers.

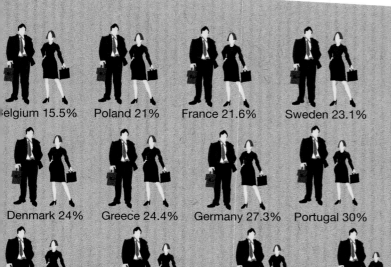

Belgium 15.5%   Poland 21%   France 21.6%   Sweden 23.1%

Denmark 24%   Greece 24.4%   Germany 27.3%   Portugal 30%

Netherlands 30.4%   United Kingdom 38.6%   Czech Republic 39.8%   Hungary 47.8%   Austria 51.4%

IN THE WORLD:

There are **600 MILLION** illiterate women compared to 320 million illiterate men.

56 MILLION TO 60 MILLION young girls haven't received an education, compared to 48 million to 54 million boys.

This gap grows **SMALLER EACH YEAR.**
Things are progressing!

Salary differences between men and women (in %)

RELIGION

There is a great diversity of cultures, beliefs, and religions in the world. Religious beliefs have evolved during the history of humanity, and a number of religions have either disappeared or been replaced by others. Today, there are roughly 4 major types of religion. Monotheistic religions, such as Judaism, Christianity, and Islam, originated in the area around the Mediterranean. Hinduism, which is practiced in India, and the more philosophical religions, such as Buddhism, Taoism, and Confucianism, were born in eastern Asia. Finally, animistic religions, which hold that a spirit inhabits every living being, are practiced primarily in Japan and Africa, and by various peoples of Asia, Oceania, and South America. Each person might think that within his religion alone lies the truth, that his is the right one and that everybody else must follow it. But this way of thinking has been responsible for massacres throughout history. In order to live together and develop in a sustainable manner, we must accept each other's differences.

Stonehenge, Wiltshire, England

More than

85

percent of
people practice
a religion

JUDAISM, CHRISTIANITY, AND ISLAM

The Temple Mount and the Wailing Wall, Jerusalem, Israel

These three religions worship a single god, called Jehovah by Jews and Christians, and Allah by Muslims.

JUDAISM is a matrilineal religion that has existed for around 4,000 years. Jews await the appearance of the Messiah, God's envoy, who will save the world. They worship at temples and study and discuss the body of principles contained in their sacred text, the Torah.

FOR CHRISTIANS, Jesus, born about 2,000 years ago, is the Messiah sent by God. His word is founded on love, and his life was recorded in the Gospels, which the disciples are charged with spreading. There are around 1.9 billion Christians in the world: Catholics, Orthodox, and Protestants.

ISLAM was founded by the prophet Muhammad, who was born in Mecca in 570. He transcribed the message of Allah in the Koran, which stands as the text of reference for Muslims. Every good Muslim must respect the 5 pillars of Islam: the profession of faith, prayer 5 times a day, the annual fast during Ramadan, giving alms to the poor, and the pilgrimage to Mecca. There are approximately 1.3 billion Muslims in the world.

HINDUISM

Ritual bathers on the ghats (steps) of Varanasi, Ganges River, Uttar Pradesh, India

Hinduism came about roughly 5,000 years ago in the Indus Valley of India.

Hindus believe in a single god and view other deities as manifestations of that supreme god; the 3 main deities are Brahma, Shiva, and Vishnu. Ganesh is another popular deity. The Hindu religious texts, the Vedas, are probably the most ancient religious texts in the world, and they give instruction in self-knowledge. Hindus believe in reincarnation, the rebirth of a soul in a new body after death.

HINDUISM
is the world's third-largest religion, with
900 MILLION FOLLOWERS.

The practice of Hinduism is a way of life. It influences the everyday lives of more than
80 PERCENT
of the Indian population.

Brahma   Ganesh   Vishnu

BUDDHISM

The Bodnath Stupa, Buddhist temple, Kathmandu, Nepal

Buddhism was founded in India approximately 2,500 years ago by Prince Siddhartha Gautama, known as the Buddha, "the awakened one."

It is a body of philosophies and does not refer to any god. Nevertheless, as its practice involves a number of rituals, Buddhism is considered a religion. Its teachings are devoted to the development of the human spirit in harmony with nature, of which people play a part. Buddhists believe in the doctrine of rebirth, which can occur in any living being.

THERE ARE 350 MILLION TO 500 MILLION BUDDHISTS IN THE WORLD.

The Dalai Lama, the spiritual leader of Tibetan Buddhism, is an important Buddhist figure. Buddhist texts were written by various past and living masters.

Buddhist temples take in troubled children, who eventually become monks.

ANIMISM

Shinto Temple of Meiji-Jingu, Tokyo, Honshu, Japan

Animists believe that all things in nature, both animate and inanimate, have souls that live in harmony with people. Animism is practiced for the most part in the traditional societies of Africa, South America, North America, Siberia, and Oceania. It is also present in Japan, in the country's national religion, Shintoism.

Among animists, a shaman has a number of roles, such as that of a healer.

SHAMANS,

who are especially prevalent in Asia and America, are people endowed with the unique ability to communicate with the world of spirits through trance.

CONFLICTS

The number of conflicts in the world is increasing, as is their duration. The struggle for resources such as water, land, oil, or minerals is often at the heart of these wars. The inequality of riches among populations also exacerbates these tensions. The majority of today's wars are internal conflicts within a country, and 90 percent of the victims are civilians. Each year, 20 million to 40 million people seek refuge in another region of their country, or even abroad. In Chad, hundreds of thousands of people are concentrated in refugee camps planted in the middle of the desert. Children and adolescents make up nearly half of these forced migrants. The vast majority of conflicts taking place today are in Africa and Asia, most often in poor or underdeveloped countries. The developmental aid given to these countries is always meager, whereas the arms trade keeps increasing.

Sudanese refugee camps at Goz Amer, near the Sudanese border, Chad

20 MILLION TO 40 MILLION people are displaced each year within their country, or seek refuge abroad

THE EUROPEAN UNION WAS BUILT ON THE ASHES OF WAR

Oradour-sur-Glane, Haute-Vienne, Limousin, France

For centuries, Europe was torn apart by wars among its various countries.

The last one, World War II, took place from 1939 to 1945. It spread beyond the European borders to include the Union of Soviet Socialist Republics (currently Russia and its neighboring states), the United States, Japan, and many of the countries of Africa, which were at that time European colonies. This war claimed the lives of nearly 50 million people total, 30 million in Europe.

POOLING OUR RESOURCES TO ENSURE PEACE

In 1950, only 6 years after the war ended, Germany, Belgium, France, Italy, Luxembourg, and the Netherlands decided to pool their strategic resources of coal and steel. This was the founding moment of what would later become the European Union. Its first objective is to ensure peace among its member states.

MILITARY SPENDING IN BILLIONS OF DOLLARS

B-52s at the Davis-Monthan Air Force Base near Tucson, Arizona, United States

In 2006, global military expenditures reached **$1.2 TRILLION,** whereas developmental aid amounted to **$107 BILLION.**

Governments throughout the world today spend 10 times more money on military equipment than on developmental aid for poor countries.

Yet poverty, the lack of drinking water, the dearth of land, and the fight for scarce resources are at the origin of a number of wars. And when a country is at war, it thinks more about procuring weapons and recruiting soldiers than about building schools or protecting its people's access to food. Wars exacerbate poverty in already poor countries.

CHILD SOLDIERS

There are around 250,000 child soldiers in the world. They have not yet reached the age of 18, but they have been enlisted by force to fight in armed groups or serve as soldiers. The youngest are barely 10 years old. Fortunately, organizations and groups such as UNICEF (the United Nations Children's Fund) have succeeded in saving many of these child soldiers. They are cared for, given aid, and encouraged to speak about their experiences with adults. Some of them are reunited with their families. They can once again attend school or learn a trade; another life becomes possible for them.

Since 2001, more than 15,000 child soldiers each year have been saved from war.

MAKING A
LIVING

Salt is produced along the coastline by evaporating saltwater, or it can come from salt mines, which are often located in the mountains. In the old days, salt used to be a scarce, precious commodity, transported over long distances. Essential to health, it was also used to preserve food. Salt was used as a currency in China, and it is from the word *salt* that the word *salary* was derived, which, for Romans, corresponded to a sum paid to soldiers to buy salt. Today salt is cheap, and in many countries, the workers who produce it are among the poorest of the poor. The salt trade is not unlike that of a number of products, be it clothing, toys, machines, or food: What is produced in one place is often consumed in another. But salaries and labor conditions are so different throughout the world that many workers can't live properly, in rich and poor countries alike.

Sea salt drying in the saltworks at Punta Vigia, Ocoa Bay, Dominican Republic

2 BILLION people around the world earn less than **$3 PER DAY**

218 MILLION CHILDREN WORK

Brickyard east of Agra, Uttar Pradesh, India

Around the world, 218 million children and adolescents ages 5 to 17 are put to work.

Some help their parents on the farm or in the shop. But 126 million of them are subjected to the worst forms of exploitation, like prostitution, factory work, construction, mining, and domestic labor.

International associations such as UNICEF fight to free children from this cruel fate so that they grow up under the protection of their parents and go to school.

PROJECTS CREATED FOR YOUNG PEOPLE, BY YOUNG PEOPLE

Unemployment primarily affects the young people of the world, notably those who live in shantytowns. Many of them can't imagine a future outside a string of unstable odd jobs. But some young people in the favelas of Brazil decided that they deserved a better life. They created programs in which children make objects from recycled trash. Some transform plastic bottles and other forms of waste into amazing pieces of furniture, whose ecological designs sell well, and others have chosen to follow a profession in stage design. Today, these programs created for young people, by young people, are spreading all over Brazil.

FAIR TRADE

Fields near Quito, Sierra region, Ecuador

The average income of the 20 richest countries is 37 times higher than that of the 20 poorest.

The gap between the richest and poorest inhabitants of the planet is unsustainable. It has a negative effect on the preservation of the earth's resources as well as the harmonious development of humanity. To help compensate for income disparities, an economist named Frans van der Hoff started up a more equitable form of business: Thanks to a label (the Max Havelaar label), consumers know that they are buying a product whose producer was paid a decent wage.

FAIR TRADE MEANS:

- 1.4 MILLION PRODUCERS AROUND THE WORLD
- MORE HOSPITALS AND SCHOOLS IN COMMUNITIES

POVERTY IN RICH COUNTRIES

In rich countries as well, the number of people who don't make enough money for housing, food, and medical care is increasing. In the United States, for example, 45 million people do not have health insurance. In France, it's possible to work and still not be able to afford housing. That's how it is for one-third of the country's homeless. What's more, certain diseases that we once thought were eradicated in rich countries, such as scurvy, which is caused by a lack of vitamin C, are starting to resurface among the very poor.

BEING AN
ACTIVE CITIZEN

Recent decades have seen the rise of private, nongovernmental organizations (NGOs) dedicated to making the world a better place. They can be local, national, or international agencies whose goal is to defend the rights of certain groups, such as people with disabilities. Some protect the environment, or channel their aid into humanitarian causes. The French-based organization Aviation Without Borders (Aviation Sans Frontières), for example, is a group of pilots who offer their services and their free time to distribute medical supplies to the most remote areas of the world, or to escort sick people.

NGOs play an extremely important role in the world. For example, they speak with the government and question businesses when they engage in harmful practices toward the environment or don't properly respect their employees. By joining such organizations, we can make a difference in the world and promote justice, solidarity, and respect for nature.

Aviation Without Borders mission in Casamance, Senegal

There are
more than
37,000
NGOs
around the world

ASSOCIATIONS THAT DEFEND THE ENVIRONMENT

Flamingoes on Lake Nakuru, Kenya

Preserving natural habitats and wild species isn't easy.

Doing so requires communicating with the government, working with local populations, and even confronting large multinational corporations wanting to acquire land to build a mine or produce palm oil or soybeans. Only very organized associations, formed by local populations or on the national or international scale, are equipped to do the job. Thus, joining an association, and supporting petitions and actions toward a just cause, is one of the best ways to protect the earth.

DID YOU KNOW?

The 9 biggest environmental organizations active in Europe (which include the World Wildlife Fund, Greenpeace, and Birdlife) have a total of approximately 20 million members.

The orphanage of Nairobi takes in young elephants whose mothers were killed.

COMING TOGETHER TO SAVE OTHERS

"10,000 Hearts for a Red Ribbon," Le Mans, Sarthe, France

How do you show your solidarity with people who live on the other side of the planet?

HIV/AIDS: A DISASTROUS EPIDEMIC

Since the early 1980s, HIV/AIDS has killed more than 28 million people. During 2006 alone, 2.9 million died, of whom 38,000 were children, and 4.3 million individuals were infected. This brings the number of people infected to 39.5 million. Sub-Saharan Africa is the primary seat of the epidemic. Every 5 years, a dozen countries in this region lose 10 percent of their active adult population to HIV/AIDS.

By joining an organization! Above, as part of "10,000 Hearts for a Red Ribbon," nearly 6,000 men, women, and children came together to form an immense heart, which was then photographed for a postcard.

Proceeds from the sale of the postcard went toward the fight against AIDS, a disease caused by the HIV virus. The disease weakens the human immune system, leaving infected people vulnerable to many illnesses. Eventually, the body is unable to defend itself from diseases.

PART 7

FOOD

WORLD AGRICULTURE

To a person from an industrialized country, this image of fields being tilled by hand must look like something from the past. Yet it represents the most common form of agriculture, one that is still practiced today. Worldwide, 80 percent of farmers cultivate their fields by hand. The more fortunate ones have animal-drawn plows, but they are few—only 1 out of 5 farmers. And finally, a tiny minority have access to one or several tractors: fewer than 1 out of 50 farmers. With a tractor, a farmer can cultivate nearly 500 acres alone, which would otherwise require the work of several families. Thus farmers in poor countries, who work by hand and lack the fertilizers and pesticides needed to increase their production, find themselves helpless in the face of the massive production of industrialized countries. To understand agricultural issues, one must first acknowledge the differences between farmers around the world.

Working in the fields north of the island of Phuket, Thailand

AGRICULTURE EMPLOYS half the men and women **ON THE PLANET**

INDUSTRIALIZED AGRICULTURE IS PRACTICED BY A SMALL PERCENTAGE OF FARMERS WORLDWIDE

Harvest time in the fields of the Beauce region, Eure-et-Loir, France

To make room for tractors, farmers in the Beauce region of France uprooted hedges to enlarge their fields.

This way, they could harvest their crops over a period of just several days. But this landscape could just as easily be the great grain-producing regions of Ukraine, Russia, the United States, Canada, or Australia. Or even those of South America, cleared from the Amazon forest.

Thanks to these agricultural tools, farmers in Beauce—one of the biggest agricultural regions in Europe—expend 1,000 times less labor to produce 1 pound of wheat than a farmer working by hand!

CROPS ARE CUT AT THE SAME LENGTH TO MAXIMIZE PRODUCTION

All the wheat is level—no marguerite, cornflower, or poppy raises its colorful head above the uniform spikes. This means that the planted grains were specially selected to produce in great abundance. Pesticides and fertilizers were spread about to prevent other plants from growing, isolate destructive elements, and maximize yields.

MANUAL AGRICULTURE IS PRACTICED BY 80 PERCENT OF FARMERS WORLDWIDE

Farmers near the Buyo Dam, Ivory Coast

The small farmers of the world are suffering as a result of the rise of industrialized agriculture in North and South America, Europe, Russia, Australia, and elsewhere.

Using only manual tools on small parcels of land, they cannot compete with mechanized farmers. As a result, they become more impoverished year after year and have more and more difficulty meeting the needs of their families. Fair trade was created to protect these kinds of producers.

850 MILLION PEOPLE THROUGHOUT THE WORLD SUFFER FROM HUNGER. TWO-THIRDS OF THEM COME FROM FARMING FAMILIES.

Farmers grow crops on small parcels of land farmed by hand.

125

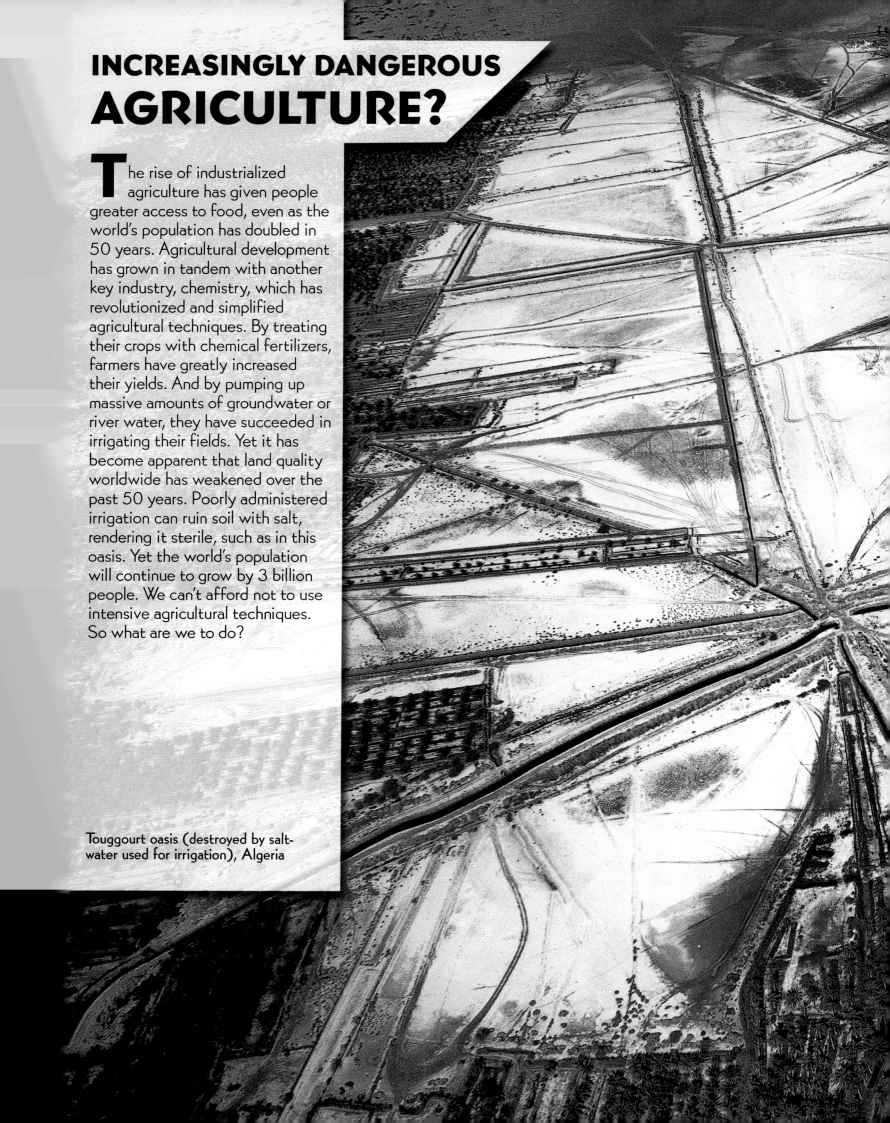

INCREASINGLY DANGEROUS
AGRICULTURE?

The rise of industrialized agriculture has given people greater access to food, even as the world's population has doubled in 50 years. Agricultural development has grown in tandem with another key industry, chemistry, which has revolutionized and simplified agricultural techniques. By treating their crops with chemical fertilizers, farmers have greatly increased their yields. And by pumping up massive amounts of groundwater or river water, they have succeeded in irrigating their fields. Yet it has become apparent that land quality worldwide has weakened over the past 50 years. Poorly administered irrigation can ruin soil with salt, rendering it sterile, such as in this oasis. Yet the world's population will continue to grow by 3 billion people. We can't afford not to use intensive agricultural techniques. So what are we to do?

Touggourt oasis (destroyed by salt-water used for irrigation), Algeria

Nearly one-third
of arable land
**HAS BEEN
ABANDONED**
in the last 40 years

PESTICIDES KILL NEARLY 20,000 FARM WORKERS EACH YEAR

Treating carrots with pesticides on Jeju-do Island, South Korea

Humans aren't the only ones who reap the benefits of their crops. Many organisms, such as insects and molds, feed off them as well.

Ever since people began tilling the land, they have sought ways to ward off the pests that destroy their crops. They have also uprooted wild plants that suck nutrients away from crops. Fifty to seventy years ago, the chemical industry started to produce pesticides that kill these destructive elements. Today we realize that pesticides have many negative effects on people and their environment. A number of countries have started to encourage their farmers to reduce the use of pesticides.

GMOs

GMOs are genetically modified organisms, whose molecules have been altered to generate new traits in an unnatural way. Some GMOs are developed to improve the quality of food within communities. But these are rare. Nowadays, 99 percent of GMOs are created by big companies to synthesize pesticides or resist them. And 90 percent of them do not even affect crops grown for human consumption. That's why ecological organizations and farmers often criticize their use.

PROBLEMS CAUSED BY MONOCULTURE

Agricultural landscape near Pullman, Washington, United States

Monoculture is the practice of growing a single crop year after year over the same area.

It's a goldmine for pests: Their food of choice extends out as far as the eye can see! And no bird can distract them, because the hedges have disappeared. To make ends meet, a farmer must increase the doses of pesticides on crops. Monoculture ruins soil, since it is always the same nutrients that get depleted, requiring even more fertilizer. When used excessively, these fertilizers can seep into rivers and eventually the sea, which provokes the growth of multitudes of algae detrimental to fish.

PRODUCTIVE AND GREEN FARMING IS POSSIBLE

To grow crops in a more ecologically minded way, it's best to diversify the crops one grows and never let the land be exposed. This allows the soil to be revived and restores its nutrients. It also makes crops less vulnerable to pests. What's more, thanks to new agronomic techniques, it's still possible to be productive, and this is crucial, because in the future, we will have to be able to feed 9 billion people!

THE PROBLEM OF
MEAT

In 50 years, meat consumption has multiplied 5 times worldwide, whereas the population has only doubled. Consumed primarily by the inhabitants of rich countries, or the richest people living in poor countries, meat, when eaten in excess, poses a number of ecological problems. Livestock farming is responsible for 18 percent of greenhouse gas emissions, which cause climate change. Industrial livestock farming requires a significant amount of grains, which are taken away from communities that need it to eat. Thus, 40 percent of grain marketed in the world is given as feed to animals. In addition, animals are often raised in deplorable conditions, which affect their health and call into question their suitability for food. Excess consumption of meat also isn't good for humans: It increases a person's likelihood of contracting a number of diseases, such as heart disease, obesity, and certain cancers. The evidence speaks for itself: To preserve our planet and its health, prosperous countries must consume less meat.

Feedlot on the outskirts of Bakersfield, California, United States

Nearly 2,000 GALLONS of water are needed to produce 1 pound of beef

131

GRAIN FOR ANIMALS

Wheat field, the polder of Mandi, Chad

40 percent of commercial grains in the world are used to feed animals. Meanwhile, 850 million people on the planet are starving.

Grains are delicate crops that require good land in order to grow. They have always served as the staple food for humankind. The least fertile lands were reserved for animals that could feed off grasses. But today, increased meat consumption has made breeders want to accelerate the growth of their cattle. To do this, they feed them grains.

That's why nowadays the most fertile lands are not dedicated to feeding people, but animals!

EVERY MONTH, A BREED OF LIVESTOCK DISAPPEARS IN THE WORLD

Because livestock farmers want to increase production, they prefer more productive breeds and have given up raising older and more local breeds, which are disappearing. Because these disappearing breeds possess qualities that could be useful to us in the future, scientists are trying to conserve them by freezing their embryos. But this method is far less effective than simply continuing to breed them!

DEFORESTATION IN THE AMAZON

Deforestation in the Amazon, Mato Grosso do Norte, Brazil

Soybean crops used for meat production are the primary cause of deforestation in the Amazon.

Soybeans have become the staple feed for chickens, pigs, and cows in industrial livestock farming. Soybeans contain a lot of protein that complements the nourishment provided by grains. Countries such as Brazil and Argentina decided to invest in soybean production, and to do so, they have cut down swaths of the Amazon forest to create farmland. As a result, soybeans have become the primary cause of deforestation in the Amazon! By decreasing our meat consumption, we can help protect the forests of the Amazon.

ON THE PLANET:

• There are between 1 and 1.5 billion head of cattle on the planet. Their combined weight is greater than that of human beings!

• Each year, 45 billion chickens are farmed and consumed.

• And that's nothing compared to the production of pigs; pork is the most commonly consumed type of meat.

Confined to cages, laying hens never see sunlight.

CLIMATE

PART 8

THE CONSEQUENCES OF CHANGE

All over the planet, the climate is changing. The atmosphere's temperature is rising. Glaciers perched along mountaintops are melting. The ice floe that forms during the winter when the Arctic Ocean freezes has lost 60 percent of its depth in 40 years. The lives of polar species, such as polar bears, are endangered. Communities of people, such as the Inuit, are leaving their villages. Currents have changed direction in the sea; in the atmosphere, wind patterns have been disturbed. The sea level is rising along the coastline, threatening lowlands. On the continents, natural disasters related to climate change, such as floods, droughts, hurricanes, and fires, are multiplying. The number of victims of these disasters increases the more that humans disturb their environment. When we enlarge cities, we prevent soil from absorbing water, which intensifies flooding. When we cut down trees, we promote the destructiveness of wind velocity, because there are no longer any forests to act as windbreakers. The climate is changing, and our behavior is, in large part, to blame. Altering our behavior is crucial!

Broken ice barrier near the Turku archipelago, Finland

Global temperatures could increase
3.5°F TO
11.5°F
this century

RISING TEMPERATURES MAKE FORESTS MORE VULNERABLE TO FIRES

Seta Valley, destroyed by fire in August 2007, Euboea Island, Greece

In 2007, Greece experienced the worst fires in its history when nearly 450,000 acres of forest went up in smoke.

In the Mediterranean region, in California, in Australia—fires have broken out in many places in the last few years. Humans are directly responsible: cigarette butts, barbecues, and campfires are among the principal causes. But rising temperatures and droughts make forests even more vulnerable; they can be set ablaze in the blink of an eye. So one must be doubly cautious when walking through these areas in the summertime.

THE EFFECTS OF CLIMATE CHANGE ON WILD SPECIES

As average temperatures rise, climatic patterns shift, which affects the species in each region. In the Mediterranean, for example, the cork oak is slowly giving way to the cedar of Lebanon.

For some species, the consequences are grave. For example, some species of birds can no longer find food in the springtime, because insects are no longer developing during the same time. Climate change can therefore threaten a quarter of the earth's species in the course of the century.

CLIMATE REFUGEES

Flooded houses south of Dhaka, Bangladesh

Global warming leads to rising sea levels and larger amounts of rainfall during the rainy season.

For Bangladesh, that's a double threat. The country's low-lying lands are threatened by rising seas, and the many rivers that cross the country flood often. Twenty million Bangladeshis could be displaced by 2020 due to the continuous inundation of their land. They would be climate refugees, people forced to leave their homes because of climate change.

WE ARE ALL AFFECTED

The number of climate-related disasters has quadrupled in 20 years. Floods, hurricanes, typhoons, droughts—these natural disasters, linked to climate change, haven't stopped increasing. No continent is spared, but the number of victims is higher in poor countries that are less equipped to help and treat affected areas.

BY 2050, AS MANY AS 135 MILLION PEOPLE MAY BE FORCED TO LEAVE THEIR LAND BECAUSE OF CLIMATE CHANGE.

WHY?

To understand the causes of climate change, governments around the world have called upon their best scientists. They all agree: The most likely cause of climate change is human activity. Human activity emits large amounts of greenhouse gases. But not all countries are equally responsible; it's the richest countries in the world that emit the most.

Humans have strived to improve their comfort, which is normal. The building of more spacious homes, far from city centers, meant that homeowners had to buy cars. In several decades, this gave rise to immense suburbs whose inhabitants consume vast amounts of energy getting around, heating their homes, and constructing new buildings. That's why a person living in Phoenix, Arizona, which is fairly spread out, consumes roughly 7 times more energy than a person living in Paris and 35 times more than a person in Hong Kong! To learn how we can help our climate, we must first become aware of our actions and habits, and figure out which are responsible for emitting the most greenhouse gases.

Highlands Ranch in the suburbs of Denver, Colorado, United States

If global temperatures increase more than **3.5°F**, the climate could spiral out of control

WHAT IS THE GREENHOUSE EFFECT?

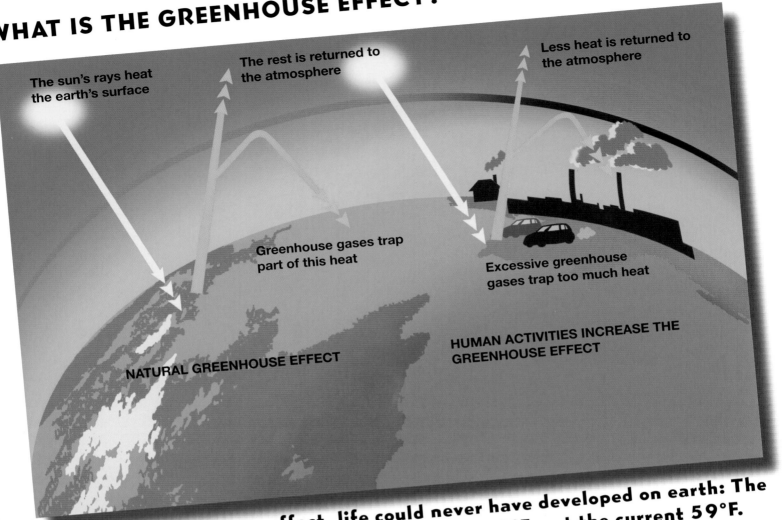

The sun's rays heat the earth's surface

The rest is returned to the atmosphere

Less heat is returned to the atmosphere

Greenhouse gases trap part of this heat

Excessive greenhouse gases trap too much heat

NATURAL GREENHOUSE EFFECT

HUMAN ACTIVITIES INCREASE THE GREENHOUSE EFFECT

Without the greenhouse effect, life could never have developed on earth: The average temperature would be slightly less than 0°F, not the current 59°F.

The atmosphere is made up of gases, such as carbon dioxide (CO_2), water vapor (H_2O), methane (CH_4), and others, that have the ability to trap heat. So when the earth, warmed by the sun's rays, releases its heat, these gases trap a portion of it. But human activity generates too much greenhouse gas. When in excess, greenhouse gas retains too much heat, temperatures rise, and the climate changes.

The 4 largest individual emitters of greenhouse gases are:

Consumer goods

Housing (heat, electricity, construction)

Food

Transportation

WHERE DO GREENHOUSE GAS EMISSIONS COME FROM?

Terminal 2, Charles de Gaulle International Airport, Paris, France

Transportation, which uses petroleum as a fuel, accounts for 17 PERCENT of greenhouse gas emissions in the world.

Petroleum is a combustible fossil fuel that emits plenty of CO_2. The airplane is the mode of transportation that consumes the most petroleum. A round-trip voyage from Paris to New York is equivalent to a person's carbon quota for an entire year! The airplane has allowed people all over the world to get to know each other better. But it must be used wisely. With rising petroleum prices, flying will cost even more in the future.

CARBON CREDIT

To prevent the increase in the greenhouse effect, every inhabitant of the planet should emit no more than 1,014 pounds of carbon* per year.

Today:
• an American emits an average of
10 TO 12 TIMES MORE
than that figure

• a European emits
3 TO 6 TIMES MORE

• a Chinese person emits **2 TIMES MORE**

We must reduce our emissions and abandon technologies that pollute the most!

*Equivalent to 1.87 tons of CO_2 or 178 pounds of methane (CH_4)

DEFORESTATION

Deforestation is responsible for 22 percent of greenhouse gas emissions in the world!

When forests are slashed and burned, all the carbon stored in trees for decades, even centuries, is released. This carbon immediately increases the quantity of greenhouse gases in the atmosphere. This is why, after China and the United States, Indonesia emits the third-highest level of greenhouse gases in the world. Its population is smaller and poorer, but the country burns the equivalent of nearly 300 football fields per hour!

GREENHOUSE GASES ON MY PLATE!

Tomato cultivation near Tepic, Nayarit state, Mexico

In industrialized countries of the northern hemisphere, which is to say in Europe, the United States, Canada, and Japan, tomatoes grow only during summer.

Yet we eat tomatoes all year long. To do so, we import them from warm, faraway countries. Northern Europe imports them from the Maghreb (Morocco, Algeria, and Tunisia) or southern Europe, and the United States and Canada get theirs from Mexico and other countries in Latin America. We also grow them in greenhouses. But transportation and the heating of greenhouses emit a high number of greenhouse gases. What's more, agricultural workers employed in these farms are often paid low wages. What's wrong with waiting to eat fruits and vegetables until they are in season?

DID YOU KNOW?

• **A FRUIT IMPORTED BY AIRPLANE** requires 10 to 20 times more fuel than the same fruit produced locally in season: 2 pounds of strawberries in the winter requires the equivalent of 1 gallon of diesel fuel to arrive on your plate.

• **PRODUCING 2 POUNDS OF BEEF** expends the same amount of energy as a 43-mile car ride.

• **FROZEN FOODS** and prepared foods require the emission of a lot of greenhouse gases. A lot of energy is required to store them, package them, and ship them.

ENERGY PRODUCTION IS THE PRIMARY SOURCE OF GREENHOUSE GAS EMISSIONS

Jänschwalde power station near Peitz, Brandenburg, Germany

Energy production is responsible for 27 percent of world emissions. The majority of power stations run on coal, a combustible fossil fuel that emits a high amount of carbon dioxide.

Hydroelectricity from dams emits less, but their reservoirs release methane, another harmful greenhouse gas. Nuclear power plants have replaced coal with uranium and emit far fewer greenhouse gases. But nuclear power produces very dangerous radioactive waste, and uranium resources, much like those of coal, are limited. So, whether it's for the sake of the climate or to prevent fuel from running out, we should all save electricity and rethink our modes of production.

PRODUCING GOODS AND SERVICES

Industry generates 25 percent of greenhouse gas emissions.

The manufacturing of goods that we use on a daily basis—from home products, to your backpack, to the car your parents drive—is responsible for a quarter of greenhouse gas emissions in the world. This is one of the reasons China emits so many greenhouse gases nowadays: It produces a large part of the goods consumed in the world.

WHAT WE CAN DO

We can each play a part in reducing greenhouse gas emissions and participate in the fight against climate change. Some actions require mobilization at the level of government or industry, but by contributing as individuals—children as well as parents—we can do what is right and encourage government officials and business owners to act for the future of our planet. For example, shoppers can opt to buy fruits and vegetables when they are in season and sold without packaging. They can ask the vendor whether the food was produced locally. We should think about all our purchases this way and choose to recycle, repair, and reuse, rather than throw out and buy again. We can try to reduce our energy consumption at home and in the car. We can even, simply on our own, avoid contributing to world deforestation and encourage preserving our forests. It's not so complicated, and after all, for the sake of our planet, the difference is inestimable!

Aligre Market in the 12th Arrondissement of Paris, France

TO HELP PROTECT THE CLIMATE, we must buy locally

TO PRESERVE OUR CLIMATE, WE MUST PROTECT OUR FORESTS!

Tree plantation near Seix, Pyrenees, France

Attempts are being made to replant trees on the bare summits of the massive Pyrenees, located between France and Spain.

It's not easy: A forest planted by humans is never as rich as a natural forest. The massive deforestation that has taken place on our planet over an entire century is a catastrophe. Unfortunately, many governments are complicit. Action depends first and foremost on the mobilization of citizens.

People often plant trees for the benefit of future generations.

A LABEL THAT PRESERVES THE FOREST AND ITS INHABITANTS

Organizations can protect our environment. The Forest Stewardship Council (FSC) has created a label that guarantees that all wood carrying the label comes from a well-maintained forest. If all of us expressed an interest in buying wood labeled by the FSC, logging companies would have the incentive to qualify for this label and therefore preserve the forest. It would also incite governments to make this certification mandatory.

REPLACING COAL WITH RENEWABLE ENERGY SOURCES

Stripped mountains north of the city of Comendador, on the border between the Dominican Republic and Haiti

Coal is used by 40 percent of the world's population for heating, which directly contributes to deforestation.

Replacing coal with solar energy equipment, therefore, has a double advantage: It fights deforestation and reduces greenhouse gas emissions.

Today, organizations are advocating that individuals and businesses compensate for the carbon they emit. The principle is simple: Money would be given to an organization that calculates the quantity of carbon emitted, for example, during a trip. Armed with this money, the organization can then finance a project that saves an amount of greenhouse gases equal to those that were emitted. This is how communities and villages will be able to give up coal and begin to rely on renewable energy sources instead.

PLANT A TREE!

Every year, the United Nations Environment Program launches a Plant for the Planet: Billion Tree Campaign. In 2007, more than 1.5 billion trees were planted around the world!

ANYONE CAN PARTICIPATE.

SAVING ENERGY AT HOME

1: Use energy-saving lightbulbs in every room of the house

2: Turn the lights off in unoccupied rooms

3: Keep the thermostat at 66°F during the day, 61°F at night

4: Turn off all appliances at night

5: Ride your bike for short trips

6: Avoid overly packaged products

At home, you can find daily ways to reduce greenhouse gases and save the planet's resources.

For example, you can ask your parents to install long-lasting lightbulbs, which use up to 5 to 6 times less energy than normal lightbulbs. And don't forget to switch off the lights when you leave a room! Cut down on using hot water, since heating it requires energy. At night, shut off all your appliances. Avoid buying individually wrapped, overly packaged snacks, since a lot of energy is spent on manufacturing the packaging. And if you feel cold during the winter, put on a sweater instead of turning up the heat!

Renewable energy sources are plentiful and available everywhere on the planet.

Wood from permanent forests

Geothermal power

Small dams

Windmills and solar panels

Biogas factories

TRANSPORTATION CAN CONSUME LESS

Playground at Beit She'an, Galilee, Israel

There are more than 800 million vehicles in circulation throughout the world, concentrated mostly in industrialized countries.

In Europe, 80 percent of goods are transported by truck. To reduce greenhouse gas emissions, part of the trip can be made by train or boat. And let's not forget that by buying products produced locally, we reduce the need for shipping goods!

The more public transportation between and within cities becomes available, the more we can each leave the car in the garage or parking lot. For short trips, forget the car: It's so much better to walk or ride a bike! When you become an adult, you'll probably work from home more often than your parents ever did; this is called "telecommuting." So many ways of saving energy on transportation have yet to be explored!

DIFFERENT CARS

Cars must also evolve. For cars to consume less fuel, they must be built smaller. Some new models run on electricity and even compressed air! Fuel can even be derived from the fermentation of household waste. This is already being done in China and Europe. On the other hand, the use of biofuels isn't a solution, yet.

DID YOU KNOW...

THE MOST POPULATED COUNTRIES in the world are China (1.3 billion inhabitants), India (1.1 billion), the United States of America (304 million), Indonesia (228 million), and Brazil (191.3 million).

THE LEAST POPULATED COUNTRY is Swaziland, which has 1 million inhabitants.

China and India alone account for **MORE THAN ONE THIRD OF THE WORLD'S POPULATION.**

HONG KONG AND SINGAPORE ARE THE MOST URBANIZED COUNTRIES IN THE WORLD. One hundred percent of their populations live in the city. No countryside exists in these highly populated city-states. They have no choice but to expand outward, toward the sea or the sky, by building high-rises. The next most urbanized countries are Kuwait, a desert country; the little island of Puerto Rico, bordered by the sea; and Belgium, where countryside exists but is inhabited by less than 3 percent of the population.

THE COUNTRY WHOSE POPULATION IS GROWING FASTEST is the Republic of East Timor: Each year, this country's population grows by 5.5 percent. Does that figure appear small to you? At that rate, the country's population will double in 13 years!

CONVERSELY, UKRAINE'S POPULATION DIMINISHES BY 1 PERCENT EACH YEAR. Couples are no longer having enough children. The countries of the former Soviet Union are the most affected by this phenomenon.

UGANDA IS THE COUNTRY MARKED BY THE HIGHEST NUMBER OF CHILDREN: 1 out of 2 inhabitants is less than 15 years old! This is followed by Niger, Mali, Burkina Faso, and Congo, where children under 15 make up 47 to 48 percent of the population. Africa is the youngest continent in the world.

EUROPE IS THE WORLD'S OLDEST CONTINENT: In Italy, 1 out of every 5 inhabitants is older than 65! Germany, Greece, and Belgium also have a high number of people over 65, who represent 17 to 19 percent of the inhabitants. Outside Europe, Japan has the highest concentration of older people, on a par with Italy.

THE RICHEST COUNTRY IN THE WORLD

is also one of the smallest: Luxembourg. The average per capita income is more than $65,000 per year! This is followed by the United States and Norway (more than $40,000 per inhabitant annually).

THE POOREST COUNTRIES—Burundi, Malawi,

and Guinea-Bissau, in Africa—have a per capita income of between $640 and $700 per year.

The richest country in the world is 100 times richer than the poorest country!

THE GREATEST INEQUALITIES* BETWEEN INHABITANTS OF THE SAME COUNTRY HAVE BEEN OBSERVED IN NAMIBIA,

followed by Lesotho, Sierra Leone, the Central African Republic, Botswana, and South Africa. What these countries have in common is that they are mineral-rich and have vast diamond mines. These highly desirable resources lead to the great wealth of some, often to the detriment of others.

DENMARK IS THE COUNTRY MARKED BY THE LOWEST DISPARITY IN INCOME.*

Other champions of equality among its citizens are Japan, Sweden, the Czech Republic, and Norway. Among the richest countries, the United States, Hong Kong, and Singapore have the highest income inequality. But beware of averages: It's possible to be very poor in a very rich country!

*According to the Gini coefficient, which measures inequality of income distribution in a given country.

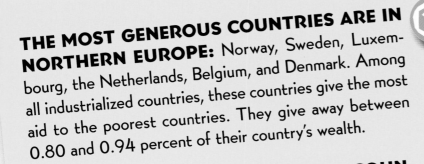

THE MOST GENEROUS COUNTRIES ARE IN NORTHERN EUROPE: Norway, Sweden, Luxem-

bourg, the Netherlands, Belgium, and Denmark. Among all industrialized countries, these countries give the most aid to the poorest countries. They give away between 0.80 and 0.94 percent of their country's wealth.

THE AWARD FOR THE STINGIEST COUN-TRIES goes to Greece, Portugal, the United States,

and Australia, which give way less than 0.25%!

THE COUNTRY OFFERING THE BEST STANDARD OF LIVING* is

Iceland, followed by Norway, Australia, Canada, and Ireland. The world's richest countries are not always the leaders in human development: Other criteria are factored in, such as access to education and health care.

THE COUNTRIES WITH THE LOWEST HUMAN DEVELOPMENT INDEX are Sierra Leone, followed by Burkina Faso, Guinea-Bissau, Niger, and Mali, all of

which are located in West Africa. These countries have been affected by lengthy civil wars, such as in Sierra Leone, or have suffered from a lack of public services, such as schools, hospitals, paved roads, etc.

*Meaning that the human development index (HDI) is highest. HDI takes into account health, life expectancy, education, and income.

DID YOU KNOW...

THE COUNTRIES THAT CONSUME THE MOST ENERGY ARE SMALL, OIL-RICH STATES:
the United Arab Emirates, Kuwait (which consumes more than 9,500 kilo-equivalents of oil per inhabitant each year*), and the islands of Trinity and Tobago in the Caribbean. Their consumption habits do not greatly affect energy consumption on a world scale since their populations are small. Canada and the United States (which consume 8,242 and 7,843 kilo-equivalents of oil per inhabitant per year, respectively) come in fourth and fifth place. But as the United States is also the third most populous country in the world, its global consumption is enormous and puts a major strain on the world energy market.

AN INHABITANT OF BANGLADESH,
on the contrary, consumes in one year what an American consumes in only one week (159 kilo-equivalents of oil per inhabitant per year). Their access to oil is insufficient.

*A kilo-equivalent of oil corresponds to the amount of energy contained in one kilo of oil. This unit of measurement allows for comparison between different forms of energy.

THE COUNTRY THAT CONSUMES THE MOST ELECTRICITY
is Iceland: Each inhabitant consumes an average of 29,430 kilowatt hours per year. The Norwegians and Canadians also consume a lot (26,657 and 18,408 kilowatt hours per inhabitant per year). They live in cold countries and have access to inexpensive renewable energy thanks to hydroelectric dams and, in the case of Iceland, geothermal power.

IN CAMBODIA AND CHAD,
on the other hand, average consumption is minute, below 10 to 11 kilowatt hours per inhabitant per year. In these countries, the vast majority of the population does not have access to electricity, just like 25 percent of the world's population.

THE COUNTRIES THAT EMIT THE MOST GREENHOUSE GASES
are China, with 6.8 billion tons of CO_2, followed closely by the United States, which emits 6.4 billion tons. Yet on an individual level, an American emits 22 tons of CO_2 per year, four times more than a Chinese person. Qatar, an oil-rich state in the Arabian Peninsula, has the highest per capita rate of greenhouse gas emissions: Each Qatari citizen emits an average of 87 tons of CO_2 per year!

POOR COUNTRIES' GREENHOUSE GAS EMISSIONS ARE MINIMAL:
The inhabitants of these countries emit an average of 66 times less CO_2 than those from richer countries. The situation is unfair: They are often the first to be affected by climate change.

IN RICH COUNTRIES,
all inhabitants have access to clean water.

IN ETHIOPIA,
only 22 percent of inhabitants, or about 1 in 5, have access to clean water. This is followed by Somalia, with 29 percent; Afghanistan and Papua New Guinea (39 percent); and Chad (42 percent). In these countries, one of the major tasks shared by inhabitants is to fetch clean water. Imagine how difficult it would be to rise out of poverty in such conditions!

THE INHABITANTS OF JAPAN AND HONG KONG LIVE LONGER THAN THE INHABITANTS OF ANY OTHER COUNTRY IN THE WORLD. Their life expectancy at birth is more than 85 years for women and more than 79 years for men. The countries of western Europe come next, where women can expect to live on average longer than 82 years, and men longer than 76. Access to medicine and maintaining a healthy diet have a direct influence on a population's longevity.

IN SWAZILAND, HOWEVER, LIFE EXPECTANCY AT BIRTH IS ONLY 30 YEARS, and it is less than 35 years in Lesotho and Botswana. These countries are greatly affected by the epidemic of AIDS/HIV. The disease is more prevalent in women: 4 women out of 10 are infected by the virus in Swaziland, and 3 out of 10 are infected in Botswana and Lesotho.

WHICH COUNTRY SPENDS THE MOST ON HEALTH? The United States, whose inhabitants each pay an average sum of $6,096 per year. It is followed by Luxembourg ($5,178 per inhabitant per year), Norway and Switzerland (about $4,000 per inhabitant per year), and Iceland ($3,294 per inhabitant per year). The countries whose health expenditure is highest are also the five richest countries of the world. The United States is unique in this club, as health is financed largely by its inhabitants and not by the state. Its system places poor people at a disadvantage.

HEALTH EXPENDITURE DOES NOT EXCEED $100 PER INHABITANT PER YEAR in 40 countries of the world, generally the poorest. For example, the Republic of Congo and Burundi spend only $15 and $16 per year, respectively, per inhabitant on health care.

THE COUNTRIES THAT DEVOTE THE MOST RESOURCES TO CHILDREN'S EDUCATION are Lesotho, which devotes more than 13 percent of its resources, and Botswana (10 percent).

THE COUNTRY THAT SPENDS THE LEAST ON CHILDREN'S EDUCATION is Equatorial Guinea, which devotes only 0.6 percent of its budget! It is followed by Indonesia and Myanmar (formerly Burma). China, despite its economic growth, spends relatively little: It comes in fifth place among countries spending the least on school, at only 1.9 percent.

JAPAN WINS THE PRIZE FOR SCHOOLING THE HIGHEST NUMBER OF CHILDREN. One hundred percent of Japanese children attend primary or secondary school. They are followed by children from France, Spain, and Norway.

THE COUNTRY IN WHICH THE LOWEST NUMBER OF CHILDREN ATTEND PRIMARY SCHOOL is Niger (40 percent), followed by Guinea-Bissau and Burkina Faso (45 percent). Even more rare than the number of children who attend primary school is the number of children who eventually attend college: fewer than 1 in 10!

GLOSSARY

Antibiotics: substances used to kill microbes.

Arid: dry; naturally lacking water.

Atmosphere: the mass of air surrounding the planet.

Bacteria: microorganisms composed of a single cell, protected by a wall. Bacteria are the first living things that appeared on earth. They are invisible to the naked eye but are present everywhere.

Biodiversity: the whole variety of living things on Earth and their natural habitats.

Biofuel: fuel obtained from plants such as sugarcane, beets, rapeseed, etc. The alcohol, esters, or oils derived from these plants serve as fuel.

Carnivorous: pertaining to organisms that eat the flesh of animals.

Climate: the prevailing meteorological phenomena—precipitation, temperature, wind, etc.—specific to a given region. Example: a tropical climate.

Coral: a kind of polyp (a small animal), or the hard, rough skeletal deposit it produces.

Deposit: a natural accumulation. Example: a copper deposit, an oilfield.

Discrimination: prejudicial treatment of people based on their gender, the color of their skin, where they live, their nationality, etc.

Domestication: the taming of an animal in order to make it serviceable to people.

Ecological: related to ecology, a science that studies the relationships between living things in their natural habitat.

Ecosystem: the community of living things inhabiting an environment and the elements (water, air, rock . . .) contained within it.

Evolution: the process by which species change and develop. The theory of evolution was first proposed by Charles Darwin, an English biologist from the 19th century.

Fertilizer: a chemical used to improve plant growth.

Fossil fuel: a source of energy found in the earth. The most commonly used are coal, oil and gas. Their combustion is one of the primary sources of greenhouse gas emissions. The formation of oil, coal, or gas deposits often takes several millions of years. These energy sources are not renewable.

Genetic: relating to genes, which transmit biological characteristics from generation to generation.

Geothermal energy: heat coming from the earth.

Greenhouse gases: atmospheric gases that absorb heat produced by the earth's radiation. Carbon dioxide (CO_2), methane (CH_4), and water vapor (H_2O) are greenhouse gases.

Ice cap: the mass of ice covering a certain region or mountain.

Irrigation: the artificial provision of water, from a river, underground source, or reservoirs.

Ore: a rock particularly rich in a metal. Example: bauxite is a rock rich in aluminum.

Overfishing: excessive fishing, resulting in rapidly depleting fish stocks.

Overgrazing: excessive exploitation of meadows, savannahs, and steppes by a high number of livestock.

Pesticide: a product that destroys insects, plants, or mushrooms that may cause damage to other plants.

Photosynthesis: the process by which plants transform the sun's rays and carbon dioxide into energy.

Plankton: microscopic living things that dwell on the ocean's surface.

Pollutant: a substance that pollutes.

Primary forest: a forest that is fully intact, and in which people did not induce any major change.

Recycle: to reuse a product or material.

Renewable energy: energy whose source is inexhaustible. This includes primarily solar energy, wind energy, and tide and wave energy.

Shantytown: a poor area of a city in which houses are made from a random assortment of materials (cardboard, sheet metal . . .) and built by their inhabitants. Shantytowns often have no system of plumbing or waste removal, nor medical centers. In Latin America, they are called *favelas*.

Sterile: free of life, or incapable of supporting life.

Toxic: being harmful to the functioning of an organism or ecosystem.

Urbanization: 1. the expansion of a city. 2. the development of an area with all the services generally available in a city, such as running water, plumbing, waste removal, medical care, police, etc. Example: urbanization of a shantytown.

Wetland: a natural area covered with both land and water. Example: a peat bog, a swamp, the banks of a lake or river, or a mangrove.

TO LEARN MORE . . .

Here is a list of Web sites where you can learn more about sustainable development, dig deeper into certain subjects, and find a plethora of useful tips. *Sites describing programs especially designed for youth are noted in italics.*

Internet sites associated with the United Nations

www.unep.org
(UNEP: United Nations Environment Program)

www.unep.org/Tunza
(*Tunza*: the youth magazine of UNEP)

www.green.tv
(greenTV: UNEP's green Web-based television network)

www.fao.org
(FAO: Food and Agriculture Organization of the United Nations)

www.ilo.org
(ILO: International Labor Organization)

www.unfpa.org
(UNFPA: United Nations Population Fund: annual report and portraits of young people throughout the world)

www.unhabitat.org
(UN-Habitat: a branch of the United Nations focused on urbanization)

www.unicef.org
(UNICEF: United Nations Children's Fund)

www.unesco.org
(UNESCO: United Nations Educational, Scientific, and Cultural Organization)

Other international sites

www.iucn.org
(International Union for Conservation of Nature)

www.ramsar.org
(Ramsar Convention on Wetlands)

www.wri.org
(World Resources Institute)

www.cites.org
(Convention on International Trade in Endangered Species of Wild Fauna and Flora)

International associations for the protection of nature

www.worldwildlife.org
(World Wildlife Fund)

www.greenpeace.org
(Greenpeace)

www.birdlife.org
(BirdLife International)

www.foe.org
(Friends of the Earth)

www.goodplanet.org
(GoodPlanet.org: a nonprofit organization dedicated to the promotion of sustainable development, chaired by Yann Arthus-Bertrand)

A number of national and local organizations work toward a more ecological and interdependent world. Your teachers, parents, members of your family, or neighbors might even be in contact with some of them: ask and find out!

INDEX

Legend